THE WELSH TABLE

First impression: March 1994
Second impression: October 1998
© Y Lolfa Cyf., 1994

The text and pictures in this book are subject to copyright
and may not be reproduced (except for review purposes)
without the prior, written consent of the publishers

Cover food photography by Adrian Wroth
Cover scenic view by Anthony Griffiths
Inside photography and illustrations by the author

ISBN: 0 86243 305 3

Printed and published in Wales
by Y Lolfa Cyf., Talybont, Ceredigion SY24 5AP
e-mail ylolfa@ylolfa.com
internet http://www.ylolfa.com/
tel. (01970) 832 304
fax 832 782

THE WELSH TABLE

CHRISTINE SMEETH

y Lolfa

THE WELSH TABLE

Contents

Introduction

There are many households in Wales where the cook sets great store in the simple, wholesome and traditional recipes passed from generation to generation. Nowhere will the visitor receive more of a welcome than at a Welsh farmhouse, inn, guest house or restaurant. If you do not live in Wales these are the places to find good home cooking served with real country hospitality.

This cookery book is not for a handful of chefs, it is cookery for everyday with recipes which are in daily use and have been down the years. The majority of the recipes in the book are simple, easy to make and delicious to eat. Some are more complicated and take a little longer but are equally appetizing and filling for the jaded palate. Buns, tea breads and scones have always been a national institution in Wales. Most have their tradition and roots firmly in the Welsh farmhouse with a combination of mouthwatering cooking and today's ideas of good food and varied country cuisine.

The food is not chic or trendy but homely, reminding us that cooks throughout the years have taken full advantage of the summer harvest, blackberries, raspberries, strawberries etc. Based on these freshest ingredients – vegetables and herbs often grown in their own gardens – with fish and meat coming from the local suppliers, here is a cookery book showing that the Welsh are renowned for the quality of their home cooked provisions.

The well-known cheeses and local breads that have made Wales famous for generations are recounted throughout this book to accompany the dishes. Such fare has its beginnings in the true Welsh joy of the love of good food and feeding people.

Most sections, for example Dinners, include starter recipes, main courses and dessert recipes. The exceptions are Breakfast, Occasional and Afternoon Tea.

I have tried to enhance the recipes with little suggestions and anecdotes of kitchen wisdom on each page to make this book of interest to everyone. Add to this some of the time-saving tips that can be gained from the use of a microwave oven and I hope you will agree that here are the essentials of the Welsh table.

Use either Metric or Imperial measures but do not combine the two.

CHAPTER 1

The Breakfast Table

CHEESE POTATO CAKE

5 potatoes, grated
2 onions, finely chopped
2 tablespoons vegetable oil
4 eggs, beaten
150ml/$^1/_4$ pint cream
100g/4 oz cheese, grated
1 tablespoon parsley, chopped
25g/1 oz margarine
Salt and pepper

Sausages are as popular now as they were when this traditional sausage making machine was an everyday sight in many Welsh butchers' shops.

Pre-heat the oven to 200C/400F/Gas mark 6. Fry the onion in the oil for 5 minutes. Transfer the onion to a bowl. Add the beaten eggs, cream, cheese and parsley to the onion.

Season with the salt and pepper. Stir well and set aside. Drain the grated potato and stir into the egg mixture. Grease a shallow ovenproof dish with the margarine. Pour in the mixture and bake for 40 minutes until crispy and brown on the top.

SMOKED HADDOCK CREAM

225g/8oz skinned and boned smoked haddock
300ml/ $^1/_2$ pint single cream
150ml/ $^1/_4$ pint white sauce
100g/4 oz breadcrumbs
$^1/_2$ level teaspoon ground nutmeg

Laverbread is usually served with a traditional Welsh breakfast.

Mince or liquidise the smoked haddock. Add the fish to the white sauce. Fold the cream, nutmeg and breadcrumbs into the mixture. Serve hot on buttered toast.

*Micro tip:
Porridge is quick from
the microwave if you
put 2 tablespoons of
oats in a cereal bowl
with milk and sugar.
Place the bowl in the
microwave for $1\frac{1}{2}$
minutes on FULL until
the mixture begins to
thicken around the
edges. Stir well,
reduce the heat to
medium for another 30
seconds and add more
milk if required. For a
change sprinkle with
cinnamon sugar and
20g raisins.

BAKED SAUSAGE BREAKFAST

450g/1 lb pork and beef sausages
100g/4 oz mushrooms
4 large tomatoes, cut in half
2 tablespoons butter
3 tablespoons freshly chopped basil

Prick the sausages with a fork and lay in a
deep oven dish. Clean the mushrooms and
cut the stalks off. Place around the sausages
in the same pan with the halved tomatoes.

Dot with small pieces of butter and sprinkle
with the basil. Bake at 200C/400F/Gas mark
6 for 30 minutes. This is a good recipe to
double up if you are cooking for a quantity of
people.

A *Welsh custom states
that only one person
must put* **bread** *into the
oven; if two people do it,
it is said they will
quarrel.*

9

GRILLED ORANGES

1 large orange per person
1 teaspoon cinnamon sugar

Vervain has always been regarded as a Holy herb with magical properties. It was supposed to hinder witches at their work and would guard the owner from any misfortune. It was also known as a soothing agent and prevented sleepless nights when taken as an infusion.

Cut the orange in half across the centre. Run a sharp knife between the segments and the peel to loosen the fruit. Take a small slice off the orange at one end and lay on a heatproof baking tray.

Grill on high until the orange is browned on the top. Sprinkle with the cinnamon sugar and serve hot.

10

STEWED PEARS WITH YOGHURT

4 large pears
75g/3 oz caster sugar
Water
1 small carton raspberry flavoured yoghurt
100g/4 oz fresh raspberries

Peel, core and quarter the pears and place them in a saucepan with the sugar and water. Let them gently simmer until tender.

Drain and place in individual serving dishes. Blend some raspberry flavoured yoghurt with the fresh raspberries and spoon over the top of the pears.

It was customary to give hens a share of all the fruit in the house on New Year's Day. It was supposed that they would lay well during the coming year.

DEVILLED LAMBS' KIDNEYS

3 lambs kidneys
25g/1 oz butter
$^{1}/_{4}$ teaspoon mustard
1 teaspoon Worcester Sauce
1 teaspoon tomato purée
1 teaspoon chopped parsley
Pinch of cayenne pepper

Slice and core the kidneys, rinse well. Fry in the butter for 5 minutes until they are cooked. Remove from the pan and keep hot.

Stir the tomato purée, cayenne, Worcester sauce and mustard into the juices and cook until thickened. Pour over the kidneys, sprinkle with the chopped parsley and serve at once.

*Micro tip:
Poached eggs are easy and quick to cook in the microwave. Put hot water and a teaspoon of vinegar in a large shallow dish. Heat on full for 2 minutes. Break the eggs on to a plate. Prick the yolks and quickly slide them into the water. Cover the dish with cling film and cook on FULL for 2 minutes. Leave to stand for 1 minute and serve on buttered toast or Savoury Welsh Griddle Cakes. (See page 12).

BACON OMELETTE

Around thirty years ago Anglesey was noted to be one enormous farm and almost entirely Welsh speaking. It was said at that time that all the corn required in Wales was grown there.

3 eggs
25g/1 oz butter
3 rashers of rindless bacon, grilled crisply

Lightly beat the eggs and season with salt and pepper. Heat the butter in a frying pan. Add the eggs and cook over a high flame. Crumble the bacon and place on one half of the omelette.

Fold over the omelette and turn it upside down in one quick movement. Cook for 1 minute and turn on to a warmed dish. Serves two.

SAVOURY WELSH GRIDDLE CAKES

225g/8 oz flour, plus 3 tablespoons
100g/4 oz margarine
1 teaspoon salt
$\frac{1}{2}$ teaspoon cayenne pepper
1 egg, beaten
2 tablespoons milk
Cooking oil

*Micro Tip:
Griddle Cakes, savoury pancakes, croissants or toast can be reheated by placing in the microwave for a few seconds and serving immediately.

Mix together the flour and seasoning in a bowl. Rub in the margarine. Add the egg and mix with a fork to form a stiff dough. Add a little milk if the dough is too dry.

Roll the dough out on a floured board until 2 cm/$\frac{3}{4}$ inch thick. Cut into rounds.

Heat and oil a griddle. Lay the cakes on carefully and cook for 8 minutes on each side. Wrap in a cloth to keep warm.

KEDGEREE

175g/6 oz long grain rice, cooked
225g/8 oz smoked haddock
4 eggs, boiled and shelled
3 spring onions, cleaned and chopped
150ml/ $\frac{1}{4}$ pint single cream
50g/2 oz butter
Salt and pepper
1 teaspoon fresh, chopped parsley
1 tablespoon milk

Poach the haddock in the milk. Skin, debone and flake it. Finely chop the eggs. Mix the fish with the eggs, rice, spring onions, cream and season with the salt and pepper.

Put the kedgeree in an ovenproof dish. Dot with the butter and cover. Bake in the oven at 180C/350F/Gas mark 4 for 25 minutes. Garnish with the chopped parsley.

*Micro tip:
Glazed ham can be cooked in the microwave. Place in a cooking dish, add water and cover with cling film. Pierce the film. Cook on MEDIUM heat at 12 minutes per 450g/1 lb gammon. Turn the gammon over halfway through cooking. Remove from the oven and allow to stand for 5 minutes. Remove the rind, score the fat and cover with the prepared glaze. Return to the microwave uncovered and cook for 3 minutes on high.

CHAPTER 2
The Lunch Table

CAERPHILLY EGGS

4 large eggs
300ml/ $^{1}/_{2}$ pint béchamel sauce
100g/4 oz Caerphilly cheese
225g/8 oz leeks

Wash the leeks very well, slice them thinly into rings. Blanch in hot water for two minutes and drain. Poach the eggs in water, shell and cut in half.

Use a plastic bucket when gathering seaweeds. A bucket is easier to use than a plastic bag which tends to split and leak.

Place two halves of each egg on individual dishes. Add the cheese to the hot béchamel sauce. Cover the egg with the sauce.

Arrange the leek rings around the edge of the dish and place under a hot grill for 3 - 4 minutes. Do not allow to burn. Serve with hot buttered toast fingers and a green salad.

*The cheapest way to obtain **crabmeat** is to buy the crabs whole, cook, clean and remove the crabmeat yourself. Frozen or tinned crabmeat is expensive. Crabs are easily cooked by dropping them into boiling, salted water and simmering for 10 minutes.*

14

BEEF, CARROT AND ONION PIE

450g/1 lb lean beefsteak
225g/8 oz carrots, cleaned and sliced
1 large onion, cleaned and sliced
225g/8 oz flour plus 1 tablespoon
100g/4 oz butter plus 1 teaspoon
50ml/2 fl oz stock
Salt and pepper
1 yolk of egg
Oil

Cut the meat into chunks and coat with the tablespoon of flour. Fry quickly in the oil to seal and add the carrots, onion and stock. Season and simmer for 20 minutes.

Rub the butter into the flour and blend in the egg. Roll out the pastry and line a greased baking dish. Spoon in the meat mixture. Roll out a pastry lid, crimping the edges of the pastry together to seal the crust.

Make a pastry decoration and brush the top of the pie with beaten egg if desired. Cook at 190C/375F/Gas mark 5 for $1\frac{1}{2}$ hours.

LAMB AND JUNIPER PIE

275g/10 oz cubed Welsh lamb
2 leeks, cleaned and sliced into rings
2 potatoes, peeled and diced
225g/8 oz button mushrooms, roughly chopped
1 teaspoon juniper berries, roughly crushed
300ml/$^1/_2$ pint beer
1 stock cube
225g/8 oz packet puff pastry
Salt and pepper
1 tablespoon tomato purée
3 tablespoons oil
2 tablespoons flour
Beaten egg, to glaze pastry

In almost every part of Wales it is considered unlucky to cut down a Juniper tree. The wood of the juniper used to be burnt on the hearth to keep away infection and an infusion made from the berries was given to cure arthritis.

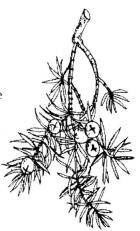

Preheat the oven to 200C/400F/Gas 6. Heat the oil in a large saucepan. Add the leeks and mushrooms and fry gently for 3 minutes. Remove and set aside.

Add the cubed lamb to the juices in the saucepan and fry until evenly browned. Stir in the flour and cook for 1 minute. Add the juniper berries, tomato purée, beer, stock cube and seasoning. Bring to the boil. Place in a casserole and cook in the oven for 30 minutes. Cool for 10 minutes.

Stir the leeks, mushrooms and potatoes into the lamb. Spoon the ingredients into a large pie dish with a rim.

Roll out the pastry on a lightly floured surface. Wet the edges of the dish. Cover the filling with the pastry, pressing the edges tightly to seal. Use the pastry cuttings to garnish if desired. Brush the pastry top with the beaten egg and stand on a baking sheet. Cook for 35 minutes until the pastry is golden brown. Serve with garden vegetables.

SAVOURY MUSSELS

*Micro tip:
For a dried fruit salad
– place the dried fruit
in a bowl with orange
juice, cover and cook
on FULL for 3 minutes.
Leave to stand
overnight and serve
for breakfast.

2 dozen (24) fresh mussels
50g/2 oz breadcrumbs
1 small onion, finely chopped
50g/2 oz butter
1 tablespoon chopped parsley
1 clove garlic, crushed

Rinse the mussels under running water and leave to soak in cold water for at least 2 hours. Place the shells in a saucepan and cover with water. Heat until the shells open, approximately 5 - 6 minutes. Remove the mussels from their shells and cook in fresh water for a further 10 minutes.

Melt the butter in a frying pan and add the breadcrumbs and chopped onion. Remove the mussels from the water and drain. Add to the pan and stir in the chopped parsley and garlic. Heat through thoroughly and serve with brown bread and butter.

18

LEEK AND POTATO SOUP

450g/1 lb potatoes
2 carrots, chopped
450g/1 lb leeks, cut into rings
300ml/ $\frac{1}{2}$ pint chicken stock
300ml/ $\frac{1}{2}$ pint milk
Salt and pepper
1 teaspoon mace

Peel and slice the potatoes. Cook the potatoes and carrots in the chicken stock for 15 minutes, add the leeks and continue cooking until all the vegetables are soft. Season to taste.

Pour into a blender and blend for a few seconds. Return to a saucepan and add the milk. Re-heat and serve with hunks of farmhouse bread.

Blackpool Mill was built of stone in 1813. The corn mill remains one of Britains finest examples of a water driven power house and commands an impressive location on the banks of the Eastern Cleddau River. It lies in the heart of Slebech Forest in the middle of Pembrokeshire National Park. It has been fully restored and can be seen in motion.

HAM AND PINEAPPLE QUICHE

175g/6 oz flour
75g/3 oz butter
2 tablespoons cold water
75g/3 oz chopped, cooked ham
75g/3 oz chopped tinned pineapple
3 eggs
300ml/ $\frac{1}{2}$ pint milk
Salt and pepper

Rub the butter into the flour, add a little salt and form into a dough with the cold water. Roll out and line a flan dish.

Beat the eggs and milk together, season with salt and pepper. Put the ham and pineapple in the flan case. Pour over the eggs and bake at 190C/375F/Gas mark 5 for 40 minutes. Serve hot or cold.

*It was once a regular custom for the cottagers and smallholders in the rural community of Dyfed to help the larger farmers at **harvest** time. In return the cottagers were allowed to grow potatoes on the farmer's land.*

19

HAM AND LEEKS IN SAUCE

*At one time young men in Wales made elaborately carved wooden **spoons**, known locally as love-spoons, and gave them to the girls of their choice as a token of their romantic intentions. These spoons can still be bought today and it is said to be lucky to hang one in the kitchen.*

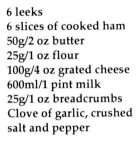

6 leeks
6 slices of cooked ham
50g/2 oz butter
25g/1 oz flour
100g/4 oz grated cheese
600ml/1 pint milk
25g/1 oz breadcrumbs
Clove of garlic, crushed
salt and pepper

Wash and trim the leeks and cook in salted, boiling water for 10 minutes. Drain and place on a warm dish. Melt half the butter in a pan and stir in the flour. Warm gently for 1 minute and slowly add the milk, stirring. Cook slowly, until the sauce thickens. Add the grated cheese and season with the crushed garlic and salt and pepper.

Wrap each of the leeks in a slice of ham and place in an ovenproof dish. Pour over the sauce. Sprinkle with the breadcrumbs and dot with the remaining butter. Place the dish under the grill until golden brown.

20

PORK PIE

900g/2lb spare rib of pork
1 teaspoon salt
Pepper
Pinch of dry mustard
3 eggs, hardboiled, plus 1 yolk, beaten
1 sachet gelatine
450g/1 lb hot water crust pastry

Trim the meat from the bones and chop finely. Put the bones into a pan with the salt and pepper, cover with water and simmer for 2 hours to make stock.

Use three-quarters of the pastry to line a greased bread tin. Half fill the pastry with the meat. Season with salt and pepper and dry mustard. Place the shelled eggs in places convenient for slicing up.

Cover with the pie lid and brush the top with beaten egg, making a hole in the top of the pastry.

Bake for 2 hours at 180C/350F/Gas mark 4. Strain the stock, mix in the gelatine and pour as much as is needed through a funnel into the pie. Serve cold.

*The **leek** is a hardy plant and is easily capable of withstanding harsh winter frosts. If planted close to carrots they help to repel carrot fly.*

*William Evans & Co, Tythe Barn Salerooms, Monk Street, Abergavenny has regular auction sales. **Cheese** moulds, cheese dishes and cake stands are typical of the specialist items often available.*

21

CAULIFLOWER AND PRAWN BAKE

*Some of the freshest
lobster and prawns
come from Shell Island.*

225g/8 oz cauliflower florettes
25g/1 oz butter
25g/1 oz flour
300ml/½ pint milk
150ml/¼ pint double cream
225g/8 oz peeled prawns
100g/4 oz Caerphilly cheese, crumbled
25g/1 oz fresh breadcrumbs
1 teaspoon tomato ketchup

Cook the cauliflower florettes until they are soft but firm. Layer them neatly into an ovenproof baking dish. Put the butter in a large pan and heat until bubbling. Blend in the flour and cook for 1 minute. Gradually stir in the milk and continue stirring until thick. Remove from the heat.

Add the prawns and cheese to the sauce, stir in the tomato ketchup and cream. Pour the mixture over the cauliflower, sprinkle with the breadcrumbs and grill until brown.

HERRINGS IN SOUR CREAM SAUCE

4 herrings
150ml/ $\frac{1}{4}$ pint sour cream
1 teaspoon mustard
Salt and pepper
1 tablespoon chopped chives
300ml/ $\frac{1}{2}$ pint water
300ml/ $\frac{1}{2}$ pint white wine vinegar

Split the herrings. De-bone the herrings by pulling off the head and back bone together.

Sprinkle the inside of the herring with salt, pepper and chopped chives, reserving a little for the garnish. Roll up from the tail end with the skin on the outside. Put the herrings in a baking pan and pour over the water and vinegar. Bake for 1 hour and leave to cool.

Goats' milk is easily obtainable throughout Wales.

Drain the fish and arrange on a serving plate. Mix the mustard with the sour cream, pour over the fish and garnish with the chopped chives.

*In Wales, the Corn Dolly was called the Hag. The **Corn Dolly** was made from the last sheaf cut from the harvest, decorated with flowers and carried home on the last waggon leaving the field. It was usually placed above the mantelpiece whilst the harvest supper was eaten and only taken down to be replaced by a new Corn Dolly the following year.*

BAKED HAM

1 large ham
3 tablespoons honey
1 cup white wine
6 cloves
1 onion, cut in half
2 bay leaves

At Llanrhidian sands, early on most mornings, you will often see a marsh pony and cart being drawn down to the mud-flats to gather cockles. (see "Richard Bell's Britain", published by William Collins, Sons & Co, Ltd. © 1981).

Soak the ham in cold water for about 8 hours or overnight. Remove any outer skin and score the fat. Put the ham in a large pan and push the cloves into the fat. Smear over the honey and pour over the wine. Put the onion halves and the bay leaves around the joint and cover with foil. Bake in a pre-heated oven at 190C/375F/Gas mark 5 for 25 minutes per 450g/1 lb.

Remove the foil 20 minutes before the joint is cooked, then continue cooking until the glaze is brown.

24

LIVER AND ONIONS

450g/1 lb lambs' liver
2 large onions, cleaned and chopped
4 bacon rashers
Oil for frying
1 tablespoon flour
Pinch of marjoram

*Micro tip:
To soak dried apple
rings put 225g/8 oz
into a shallow dish.
Pour over 300ml/$\frac{1}{2}$
pint boiling water.
Heat on FULL power
for 6 minutes. Leave
to stand for 20
minutes. Drain and
use the same day.

Remove any membrane or fatty tissues from
the liver and slice as thinly as possible. Put
the flour and marjoram into a clean
polythene bag. Place the liver in the bag and
shake gently to coat it. Heat the oil in a
frying pan and fry the liver for 4 minutes on
each side. Remove to a warm serving dish
and keep warm. Fry the onions and chop the
bacon rashers into small pieces.

Toss the rashers into the onions and continue
to fry until the bacon is crisp. Place around
the edge of the liver and serve with gravy if
desired.

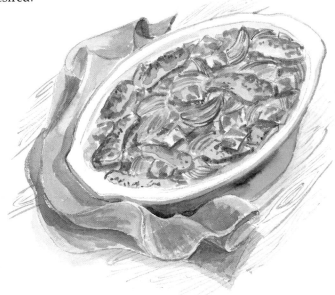

MEATBALLS

450g/1 lb lean minced beef
1 onion, finely chopped
3 tablespoons fresh breadcrumbs
1 egg, beaten
1 tablespoon fresh herbs, chopped
Salt and Pepper

Borage in the Welsh language is 'Llawenlys' which means herb of gladness and courage. The leaves and bright blue flowers can be used to add to summer drinks and the flowers are often added to salads.

Combine all the ingredients for the meatballs in a large mixing bowl. Shape the mixture into 18 balls, firmly pressing each one into a firm round.

Put them in a greased oven dish and cook in the oven 190C/375F/Gas mark 5 for 25 minutes until browned. Serve with a piquant sauce.

Almond Shortbread has been a favourite recipe in Wales for many years. It can be purchased ready made. For a real treat serve with ice cream or raspberry mousse.

26

*Many Welsh farms offer holiday accommodation. Numbers of visitors to Wales really get to know the country by staying on a **farm**. Holidays on farms provide the opportunity to taste true home cooking, many using their own beef, lamb and dairy produce.*

BEEF, APPLE AND POTATO PIE

450g/1 lb lean beef, cubed
450g/1 lb potatoes, mashed
2 large cooking apples
1 large onion
300ml/ $\frac{1}{2}$ pint beer
1 teaspoon freshly chopped mint
1 teaspoon fresh thyme
Salt and Pepper

Put the meat, herbs, salt and pepper into a casserole dish. Skin and chop the onion. Peel and slice the apple. Add both the apple and onion to the casserole and pour over the beer. Cook in a moderate oven 180C/350F/ Gas mark 4 for 1 $\frac{1}{2}$ hours.

Fork the mashed potato over the meat and return to the oven for 20 minutes until the potato is golden brown.

27

*Many trout farms offer smoked **trout** for sale for those who don't go fishing.*

MUSSEL AND COCKLE SOUP

24 cockles
24 mussels
2 carrots, chopped
2 onions, finely chopped
2 large potatoes, chopped
50g/2 oz chopped celery
2 teaspoons butter
150ml/$^1/_4$ pint milk
1 teaspoon mixed herbs.

*With a 750 mile coastline and numerous rivers and lakes, Wales boasts a superb variety of **fish**.*

Clean and scrub the shellfish, discarding any with broken shells. Boil them in a little water until they have opened. Remove from their shells and reserve the cooking liquid.

Cook the carrots, celery, onions and potatoes in the butter until soft. Add the cooking liquid from the shellfish. Cook for 20 minutes adding the cockles, mussels, milk and herbs. Simmer gently for 5 minutes.

CHICKEN WITH FENNEL STUFFING

1 medium sized chicken
Juice of 1 lemon
2 garlic cloves, crushed
75g/3 oz chopped fennel
2 tablespoons chopped parsley
4 tablespoons breadcrumbs
4 tablespoons olive oil
Salt and pepper

*Mistletoe **tea** was used for centuries in Wales to cure epilepsy, heart troubles and nerve complaints. To cut down a mistletoe-bearing apple tree was once considered to be extremely unlucky.*

Heat the oil in a large roasting pan. Set the oven at 180C/350F/Gas mark 4. Mix the breadcrumbs with the crushed garlic, chopped fennel, 1 tablespoon of the parsley and the juice of the lemon. Add seasoning and fill the cavity of the chicken.

Sprinkle the remaining parsley and some extra pepper over the bird. Roast for 1 hour 50 minutes until thoroughly cooked and the chicken is browned.

*Llanboidy is a Welsh **cheese** with added laverbread.*

EGG WHEY

300ml/$\frac{1}{2}$ pint milk
2 eggs
50g/2 oz sugar
3 slices bread, thinly sliced
25g/1 oz butter
Grated rind of 1 lemon
$\frac{1}{2}$ teaspoon ginger
$\frac{1}{2}$ teaspoon nutmeg

Heat the milk with the ginger and nutmeg. Stir in the lemon rind and leave to cool for 5 minutes. Beat the eggs with the sugar, pour over the milk and strain into a bowl.

Remove the crusts from the bread. Spread thinly with butter and line a buttered pudding basin. Pour in the custard and leave to soak for 30 minutes. Cover with greaseproof paper and foil.

Steam for 50 minutes, turn out and serve with a sweet lemon sauce.

Procter Brothers in Bedwas, South Wales have been making mousetraps since 1875. Baited with **cheese***, mousetraps have been used for many years, some more inventive and intricate than others. The Little Nipper remains one of the best sellers. Procter Brothers have a mousetrap museum worthy of a visit for those of a less squeamish nature.*

CARROT AND APPLE SOUP

675g/1½ lb carrots, washed cleaned and diced
450g/1 lb apples
1 tablespoon cooking oil
2 onions, chopped
600ml/1 pint chicken stock
1 teaspoon tomato purée
Salt and pepper
Bunch of fresh, mixed herbs

Put the carrots and onions in a saucepan with the cooking oil. Cook gently for 5 minutes. Peel, core and roughly chop the apples. Add to the pan and cook for a further 5 minutes. Add the stock, tomato purée and herbs and simmer for 20 minutes.

Cenarth on the river Teifi is a favourite with tourists. Often a coracle can be seen in use at this perfect spot.

Season, remove the herbs. Pour into a blender and liquidise until smooth. Return to the pan, re-heat and serve hot.

31

CHAPTER 3
The Afternoon Tea Table

*The 18th century watermill Felin yr Aber has produced flour for generations. The mill offers a collection of farm machinery as well as seeing the mill in action and provides an opportunity to enjoy a **picnic** beside the picturesque mill ponds and river Teifi. It is situated ¹/₂ mile off the A475, between Llanwnnen and Llanybydder.*

WHITE CHEESE FLAN

175g/6 oz savoury pastry
100g/4 oz Caerphilly, crumbled
50g/2 oz cream cheese
3 tablespoons thick cream
4 standard eggs
Salt and pepper
2 tablespoons flour
1 teaspoon lemon juice

Pre-heat the oven to 180C/350F/Gas mark 4. Line a flan case with the savoury pastry and bake blind by laying a sheet of greaseproof paper over the pastry, fill with baking beans and cook for 15 minutes.

Place the remaining ingredients in a large bowl and whisk until thick and creamy. Pour into the flan case and return to the oven for 25 minutes until set. This flan can be served hot or cold.

*For a **picnic** tea on a sunny afternoon take a walk along the Gigrin Farm Nature Trail, situated close to Rhayader on the A44.*

WELSH BUNS

450g/1 lb flour
25g/1 oz baking powder
$\frac{1}{2}$ teaspoon salt
175g/6 oz butter
175g/6 oz caster sugar
2 eggs, plus 1 egg, beaten
Milk

Dairy ice cream flavoured with pure, fresh flavourings is made in the Preselau Hills of West Wales at Mary's Farmhouse, Station Yard, Crymych, Dyfed.

Pre-heat the oven to 200C/400F/Gas mark 6. Sift the flour, baking powder and salt. Rub the butter into the mixture. Add the sugar. Mix in the eggs and enough milk to mix to a fairly stiff consistency.

Shape into buns and brush with beaten egg. Place on a greased baking tray and bake for 20 minutes.

33

FLUMMERY

*Micro tip:
More juice can be obtained from citrus fruits by microwaving them individually for 30 seconds on HIGH before squeezing.

3 tablespoons clear honey
4 egg yolks
300ml/$^{1}/_{2}$ pint sweet wine
300ml/$^{1}/_{2}$ pint double cream
2 tablespoons brandy
Thinly peeled rind and juice of 1 lemon

Put the honey, beaten egg yolks and lemon rind into a basin over a saucepan of hot water and cook until the eggs thicken and are lighter in colour. Add the lemon juice and wine, remove from the heat and stir in the stiffly whipped cream.

Traditional fishing methods are still used by many Welsh fishermen today. There is a wealth of fish and shellfish to be found around the Welsh coasts including salmon, herring, lobsters, cockles, oysters and shrimps. Around Cardigan Bay and on the Llŷn Peninsula there are small herring ports. The Quay at Conwy bustles with activity when the trawlers sail in from the Irish sea.

Whisk in the brandy and pour into a mould or individual glasses. Once set, place on a decorative plate and serve garnished with sponge fingers.

KIPPER PASTE

2 pairs kippers, boned
50g/2 oz butter
1 tablespoon double cream
1 teaspoon lemon juice
$^{1}/_{2}$ teaspoon strong black pepper, ground

Arrange kippers on a shallow dish, cover with cling film. Heat on full for 5 minutes. Remove any remaining bones and skin and leave to cool.

Mash until smooth with the butter, cream, lemon juice and pepper. Use as pâté with fresh bread or for sandwiches.

BLACKBERRY MOULD

396g/14 oz blackberries,
75g/3 oz sugar
1 sachet powdered gelatine
100ml/3$\frac{1}{2}$ fl oz water
600ml/1 pint whipping cream

Cook the fruit in a little water with the sugar
and liquidise in a blender. Dissolve the
gelatine in hot water and add to the purée.

Whip the cream until thick, reserving a little
to decorate the top of the mould, and fold into
the purée. Pour into a mould and chill for at
least 4 hours. Garnish and serve cold.

*The Rock Park **Spa** at Llandrindod Wells has 3 varieties of water on draught - saline, sulphur and magnesium. There is an exhibition centre explaining the health spas of Wales close by. Spas in Wales were fashionable at the end of the 19th century. Chalybeate Well House at Aberaeron was originally built in 1881. It is a small circular building which covers a mineral spring.*

*Micro tip:
Do not try to deep fry
in the microwave: the
oil temperature cannot
be controlled enough
to produce quality food
and it is dangerous.

HONEY BISCUITS

*According to Welsh tradition, a bush of Myrtle growing on both sides of the front door of a house brings peace and harmony for the family. Myrtle has long been regarded as a lucky plant in Britain. An **infusion** made from the leaves or a flowering sprig is said to increase beauty and induce a peaceful sleep.*

450g/1 lb flour
225g/8 oz butter
175g/6 oz honey
100g/4 oz sugar
50g/2 oz chopped mixed peel
2 eggs
1 dessertspoon nutmeg
1 teaspoon baking powder

Pre-heat the oven at 190C/375F/Gas mark 5. Sift the flour, baking powder and nutmeg into a bowl. Add the sugar.

Melt the butter and honey together in a saucepan. Pour into the flour and blend in the chopped mixed peel. Beat in the eggs.

Gather together and roll out. Cut into rounds with a cookie cutter and bake for 15 minutes.

*Kate Roberts was a well-known Welsh language writer (1891-1985). She wrote "**Tea** in the Heather" - eight linked stories of childhood in Wales at the turn of the century.*

SEED CAKE

175g/6 oz butter
225g/8 oz flour
175g/6 oz sugar
4 eggs
1 teaspoon baking powder
1 teaspoon nutmeg
1 teaspoon mixed spice
40g/1 $\frac{1}{2}$ oz caraway seeds
40g/1 $\frac{1}{2}$ oz chopped mixed peel
Icing sugar – optional

Wales is famous for its honey and the product has been used in several recipes in this book. While away an hour at the Honey Bee exhibition on the Quay at Aberaeron. Taste the honey ice-cream and visit the honey shop where you can see the bees at work in the observation hives.

Pre-heat the oven to 180C/350F/Gas mark 4. Grease and line a 900g/2 lb loaf tin. Cream the butter with the sugar until lighter in colour.

Beat the eggs into the mixture, fold in the flour adding the spices, caraway seeds and mixed peel.

Pour the mixture into a cake tin and bake in the oven for 1 $\frac{1}{2}$ hours until golden and firm to the touch. Leave to cool in the tin before turning out. Mix the icing sugar with a little water and pour over the cake if desired.

MARBLED CUSTARD

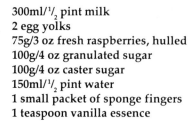

300ml/¹/₂ pint milk
2 egg yolks
75g/3 oz fresh raspberries, hulled
100g/4 oz granulated sugar
100g/4 oz caster sugar
150ml/¹/₂ pint water
1 small packet of sponge fingers
1 teaspoon vanilla essence

Boil the granulated sugar in the water for about 10 minutes until it thickens and forms a syrup. Allow to cool for 2 minutes then stir in the raspberries. Quickly pour into the bottom of two sundae dishes.

Make the custard by beating the remaining sugar and the egg yolks in a basin over hot water until the mixture is thick.

Gradually stir in the milk and continue to cook until a custard forms. Stir in the vanilla essence.

Pour over the raspberries and allow to cool in the refrigerator for 2 - 3 hours before serving with sponge fingers.

SWEET WELSH CAKES

*Delicious organic food can be sampled at the Interpretation Centre at Brynllys Organic Farm, Nr Talybont, while Bryn Cerdin Farmhouse **Cream Teas** are well-known throughout Wales. Bryn Cerdin Farm is situated on the A486, one mile north of Ffostrasol, on the New Quay to Llandysul road.*

225g/8 oz flour, plus 3 tablespoons
100g/4 oz margarine
Pinch salt
$\frac{1}{2}$ teaspoon nutmeg
75g/3 oz currants
75g/3 oz sugar
1 egg, beaten
2 tablespoons milk
Cooking oil

Mix together the flour, sugar, salt and nutmeg in a bowl. Rub in the margarine. Add the currants and egg and mix with a fork to form a stiff dough. Add a little milk if the dough is too dry.

Roll the dough out on a floured board until 2 cm/$\frac{3}{4}$ inch thick. Cut into rounds.

According to a long-lived and widespread tradition the bay tree is a fortunate plant as a protector against evil. It is said that this tree is never struck by lightning and if grown near the house it preserves those within from all kinds of infection and illness. To carry some of the bay leaves about one's person will protect the carrier from contagious diseases.

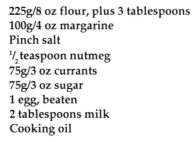

Heat and oil a griddle. Lay the cakes on carefully and cook for 8 minutes on each side. Wrap in a cloth to keep warm.

LARDY CAKE

450g/ 1 lb flour
275g/10 oz lard
50g/2 oz sugar
15g/$^1/_2$ oz fresh yeast
300ml/$^1/_2$ pint warm water
275g/10 oz lard
$^1/_2$ teaspoon nutmeg
$^1/_2$ teaspoon allspice
$^1/_2$ teaspoon salt
50g/2 oz currants and sultanas, mixed

Mix the flour and salt with the creamed yeast and water. Knead for 5 minutes, set aside until doubled in size. Knead again. Roll out the dough until 10mm/$^1/_2$ inch thick.

Dot with one third of the lard and a third of the sugar. Fold into three. Repeat this process twice more. At the last rolling out, sprinkle with the sugar, spices and fruit.

Roll out to a roughly shaped square and bake at 220C/425F/Gas mark 7 for 20 - 25 minutes until brown and crispy at the edges.

*Micro tip:
Take care when there is prolonged cooking of fat or sugar. Plastic dishes are best avoided as they tend to distort and can even burn.

41

WELSH BORDER TART

175g/6 oz shortcrust pastry
100g/4 oz sultanas
100g/4 oz raisins
100g/4 oz sugar
25g/1 oz butter
3 eggs, separated
75g/3 oz caster sugar
1 teaspoon cinnamon

*The Welsh Dresser is famous throughout the world. The North, South and Mid **Wales** regions each have their own distinctive styles. Some fine examples can be seen in a collection at the Welsh Folk Museum.*

Pre-heat the oven to 180C/350F/Gas mark 4. Melt the butter and add the sugar, cinnamon, raisins, sultanas and egg yolks. Mix well.

Line a flan ring with the pastry. Spoon in the filling and bake for 30 minutes.

Make the meringue by whisking the egg whites until stiff. Whisk in the caster sugar and pipe on to the baked flan.

Return to the oven for a further 15 minutes until the meringue is pale brown. Serve hot or cold.

ALMOND BISCUITS

175g/6 oz butter or margarine
225g/8 oz flour
225g/8 oz caster sugar
100g/4 oz ground almonds
50g/2 oz chopped almonds
1 teaspoon baking powder
Ground rice

Pre-heat the oven to 160C/325F/Gas mark 3. Rub the butter and the baking powder into the flour.

Add the sugar and ground almonds and mix to a stiff dough. Knead thoroughly with the chopped almonds.

Sprinkle a board with ground rice. Roll out the dough, 5 mm/ $^1/_4$ in thick. Cut into small rounds and prick with a fork. Bake for about 30 minutes.

*On the chapel wall in St. Julian's Chapel, Tenby is the story of the "Fishermen's Church". Many of the old fishermen's **cottages** are now boat stores. The smallest fisherman's house in Britain is on the Quay at Conwy. It is 10ft 2" high with a frontage of only 6ft and can be visited between mid March and mid October.*

GREEN VALLEY MOUSSE

4 cups finely chopped cucumber
25g/1oz unflavoured gelatine
150ml/ $^1/_4$ pint mayonnaise
2 teaspoons minced onion
$^1/_2$ teaspoon salt
2 tablespoons chopped parsley
1 cup finely chopped celery
3 tablespoons cold water

Dissolve the gelatine in the water over a low heat. Remove from the heat and stir in all the ingredients. Turn into a lightly oiled mould. Chill until firm. Unmould and garnish with triangles of buttered toast.

*Micro tip:
To loosen moulds when making a mousse or jelly, heat on MEDIUM or power 5 for 20 seconds.

CHAPTER 4

The Dinner Table

BEST WELSH SALMON

*The Coach House at Craig-y-Nos was once the home of the famous Opera singer, Madame Adelina Patti. It is now a Licensed Restaurant, Craft Centre and Tea Rooms. A speciality of the restaurant is steak, mushrooms and guinness pie. Home made **Bara Brith** and other Welsh delights are available throughout the day.*

1 salmon (sewin)
2 large carrots, chopped
2 sticks of celery, chopped
1 onion, chopped
1 lemon thinly sliced
Salt and pepper
Glass of cider or white wine

Bring the vegetables to boil in a pan large enough to accommodate the fish. Stir in the glass of cider and season well.

Wrap the fish, loosely, in a muslin cloth and place the fish in the liquid. Bring the water to the boil, switch off the heat and leave the salmon to cool in the liquid for at least half an hour.

Remove the skin while still warm and serve garnished with aspic jelly and strawberries if desired.

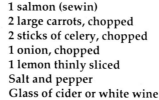

Oats were at one time the mainstay in the diet of the people of Wales and many forms of oatmeal dishes were invented including oatmeal and onion loaf (see page 80).

RICH CHOCOLATE ROLL

5 eggs, separated
225g/8 oz caster sugar
175g/6 oz plain chocolate
150ml/$\frac{1}{4}$ pint double cream
Icing sugar to finish
Cooking oil

Line a swiss roll tin with greasproof paper
and oil it well. To allow for the chocolate roll
to rise during cooking, make sure the paper
stands up 2.5cm/1 inch above the sides of the
swiss roll tin.

*In many parts of Wales it was once considered dire if any work was done in the garden or fields on Ascension Day – held 40 days after Easter. To do so would result in weak **crops** and a poor harvest.*

Beat the egg yolks and sugar until thick. Heat
the oven to 200C/400F/Gas mark 6. Melt the
chocolate in a basin over a pan of hot water
and fold into the egg mixture.

Beat the whites until stiff. Fold into the egg
and chocolate and when well mixed pour into
the swiss roll tin. Bake for 20 - 25 minutes
until firm to the touch but do not allow to
brown.

Remove from the oven, turn onto a rack and
cover immediately with a damp tea towel.
Leave to become quite cold.

Whip the cream stiffly. Turn the sponge onto
a dry tea towel and spread the cream over in
an even layer. Roll up, with the tea towel, as
this helps to stop it from cracking, and chill
for 1 hour.

*Llangrannog is a beautiful coastal village in Dyfed. For a good meal and a hearty welcome, visit the **restaurant** of Sue and Chris, Y Gegin Fach, situated overlooking the sandy beach.*

Unfold from the cloth and turn onto a serving
plate. Sprinkle with the icing sugar if desired.
A punnet of raspberries can be mixed into the
cream for a raspberry roll.

45

WELSH DUCK

1 duck
125g/5 oz small onions, skinned
450g/1 lb potatoes, cleaned and chopped
1 small swede, cleaned and chopped
125g/5 oz carrots, cleaned and chopped
Bunch of fresh herbs
Salt and Pepper

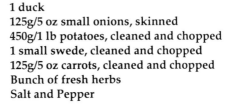

Place the duck in a large saucepan and cover with water. Simmer slowly with the herbs for 2 hours at 150C/300F/Gas mark 2.

Put the onions, potatoes, swede and carrots in the saucepan and continue cooking for 30 minutes. Drain the duck and place on a large dish with the vegetables around it, keeping the liquid to make a gravy.

MARJORAM TROUT WITH BACON

1 trout per person, cleaned and prepared
4 sprigs of fresh marjoram
1 small glass of wine
2 slices of bacon
2 slices of orange
2 rashers for each trout

Soak the orange and marjoram in the wine for an hour if possible. Put the marinated marjoram and slices of orange into the empty cavity and wrap the bacon rashers around the fish. Secure with a cocktail stick.

Grill under a medium heat until the bacon is crisp on one side. Turn the trout , baste with a little of the wine liquer and cook the other side. Serve with a crisp green salad.

TREACLE TART

175g/6 oz flour
100g/4 oz butter plus 1 teaspoon
6 tablespoons golden syrup
4 heaped tablespoons fresh white breadcrumbs
2 teaspoons finely grated lemon rind
1 tablespoon lemon juice
1 egg yolk

An 800ft high hill 'The Kymin' has views over the Wye and Monnow Valleys. The 'first gentlemen of Monmouth' built The Round House on the summit, a tower which they used as a dining club.

Rub the butter into the flour until it resembles breadcrumbs. Mix in the egg yolk with a fork and add sufficient water to make a dough. Knead the pastry on a floured surface and roll out.

Grease a shallow pie plate and line with the pastry. Prick the base lightly with a fork. Mix the other ingredients together and spread over the pastry. Roll out the pastry trimmings and cut into narrow strips. Lay the strips over the tart and trim the edges neatly.

Bake the tart in a pre-heated oven to 200C/ 400F/Gas mark 6 for 25 minutes. This tart can be served hot or cold.

ROSEMARY & HONEY LAMB

1 kg/2¹/₂ lb joint of lamb
7 or 8 sprigs of fresh rosemary
3 tablespoons runny honey
300ml/¹/₂ pint white wine
Salt and pepper

*Micro tip:
When cooking a whole
chicken, cook the bird
breast side down for
the first half of cooking
time.

Lay the rosemary in the base of the pan. Rub
the salt and pepper all over the joint and
place in a meat tin. Coat the meat with honey
and pour the wine around the joint.

Bake at 200C/400F/Gas mark 6 for 30
minutes. Baste the meat with the juices and
reduce the heat to 180C/350F/Gas mark 4
allowing a final cooking time of 30 minutes
per 450gm/1 lb.

Baste twice more during the cooking time and
add a little more wine if required. Serve with
roast potatoes, swede, broccoli.

*Crabs, lobsters and
Queen Scallops are
dredged off Aberporth,
most of which are
exported.*

A cone-shaped 2,000 ft, high hill 'The Sugar Loaf' is west of Abergavenny.

WELSH CAWL (BROTH)

600ml/1 pint lamb stock,
1 large parsnip cleaned and chopped
1 medium swede, cleaned and chopped
1 turnip, cleaned and chopped
3 large carrots, cleaned and chopped
2 sticks celery, cleaned and chopped
3 large leeks, cleaned and sliced into rings
675g/$^1/_2$ lb potatoes, cleaned and chopped
Salt and pepper
1 tablespoon fresh, chopped herbs

Put the stock into a large pan with the vegetables. Simmer for 30 minutes. Season.

Add the leeks and herbs 5 minutes before serving. Serve with chunks of fresh bread.

*Herbs that mix and complement **cheese** - basil, borage, bergamot, caraway, chives, coriander, cumin, dill, fennel, lemon balm, marigold, marjoram, mint, parsley, rosemary, sage, salad burnet, savories.*

49

APPLE AMBER

6 large apples, peeled, cored and sliced
75g/3 oz brown sugar
25g/1 oz butter plus 1 teaspoon
175g/6 oz shortcrust pastry
Pinch ground cloves
$\frac{1}{2}$ lemon
3 eggs

Herrings, once lightly smoked and slit from top to bottom then opened out are known as kippers.

Place the apples in a saucepan with the sugar, lemon rind, cloves and butter and cook until tender. Rub through a sieve, beat in the egg yolks and allow to cool.

Line a pie dish with the pastry. Pour into the pastry case. Place in the oven at 180C/350F/ Gas mark 4 for 25 minutes. Whip the whites very stiffly and spread them over the apples. Dredge a little castor sugar over the top and return to the oven to set for about 10 minutes.

*For a good basic **stock** use any bones bought or left over after a meal i.e. carcasses of chickens, veal knuckle etc. Brown the bones in the oven for 30 minutes. Transfer to a large saucepan and add 3 chopped carrots, 2 chopped onions, 1 clove garlic, $\frac{1}{2}$ bottle dry white wine and 1 large bunch fresh herbs. Cover with water, bring to the boil, then simmer for 3 hours. Skim off the top occasionally and strain through a fine sieve.*

POTATO & LAMB FRITTERS

225g/8 oz lean, cooked lamb, minced
1 onion, finely chopped
2 rashers crispy bacon, crumbled
1 clove garlic, crushed
Salt and pepper
2 tablespoons fresh thyme
450g/1 lb mashed potatoes
1 egg, beaten
2 tablespoons flour
Cooking oil

Combine the potatoes, lamb, onion, bacon, garlic, thyme and egg. Season to taste. Shape into flat cakes with the flour and cook in the oil until golden brown.

ORANGE & APRICOT MOUSSE

175g/6 oz no-need-to-soak apricots
2 oranges
3 egg yolks
50g/2 oz caster sugar
300ml/10 fl oz milk, warmed
3 level teaspoons gelatine
150ml/5 fl oz double cream

*The Bodysgallen Hotel 2 miles north of Llandudno, is a dignified 600 year old house with 7 acres of cultivated gardens including a 17th century knot garden filled with many varieties of scented **herbs**. The hotel has a good reputation for its traditional cooking.*

Pare the rind of the oranges and place in a bowl with the apricots. Cover with cold water and leave to soften for at least 3 hours. Transfer to a saucepan and bring to the boil, cover and simmer for 15 - 20 minutes. Cool.

Beat the egg yolks and sugar together. Pour on the warmed milk, return to the pan and cook slowly until the mixture thickens to a custard. Drain the apricots and orange rind.

Place in a processor or blender with the custard and the juice from the oranges. Blend until smooth.

Sprinkle the gelatine over 3 tablespoons water. Leave to soak until spongy then dissolve over a pan of hot water. Whisk the cream until thick. Stir the cream, gelatine and apricot mixture together. Pour into a ring mould and leave to set.

Turn out and decorate with piped whipped cream and a few strands of orange rind. Serve with single cream if desired.

*Organic **Muesli** is available from the Hay-on-Wye Factory, and many local shops.*

DOUBLE CHEESE SOUFFLÉS

75g/3 oz butter plus 1 tablespoon
75g/3 oz flour
450ml/³/₄ pint milk
300ml/¹/₂ pint double cream
6 eggs, separated
Salt and pepper
350g/12 oz grated cheese

Pre-heat the oven to 190C/375F/Gas mark 5.
Melt the butter in a saucepan, add the flour
and cook for 3 minutes, stirring. Blend in the
milk and season. Bring to the boil and add
half the grated cheese. Stir for 4 - 5 minutes.

Pour the mixture into a bowl and allow to
cool for 3 minutes. Stir in the egg yolks.
Whip the whites until stiff and fold into the
mixture. Pour into buttered soufflé moulds,
place in a baking dish in 12ml/¹/₂ inch water
and bake for 20 minutes. Cool until required.

*Shell Island as its name suggests is particularly good for finding pretty shells on its beach; it is also known to have over 160 different types of flowers and **herbs**.*

Cover with the rest of the cheese. Pour over
the cream and cook again for 20 minutes at
220C/450F/Gas mark 7.

*A little known custom of Wales took place on All Souls' Eve (1st November) when soul **cakes** were collected from house to house and offered to the priests who then said a prayer to give hope for the souls of the poor to come out of purgatory.*

MOTHER'S BAKED APPLES

4 large cooking apples
100g/4 oz mincemeat
1 tablespoon brandy
15g/$\frac{1}{2}$ oz butter
Lemon juice
Water

Set the oven at 180C/350F/Gas mark 4. Make a 2.5 cm/1 inch hole in the centre of each apple and remove the core. Brush the centre hole with a little lemon juice to stop it from going brown.

Grease an ovenproof dish and put in the apples. Spoon half the mincemeat into the hole in the apple. Pour a little of the brandy into each hole. Top with the remaining mincemeat.

Put a small knob of butter on top of each apple and a little water in the base of the dish. Bake for 25 minutes and serve hot with cream.

* Micro tip: when cooking cakes in the microwave leave them to cool for 2 hours and then wrap in foil and keep in the fridge. Remove an hour before serving. Return any remaining cake to the fridge after serving.

RABBIT WITH LENTILS

1 rabbit, jointed
175g/6 oz lentils
2 onions, chopped
2 carrots, sliced
2 large potatoes, peeled and chopped
1 small tin sweetcorn
25g/1 oz flour
25g/1 oz butter
Few sprigs fresh thyme
Few sprigs fresh parsley
1 bay leaf
Salt and pepper
Chicken stock to cover
Chopped parsley to garnish

*There are a great many working water mills in Wales - some more recently restored than others. Penegoes has a working **water mill** with a goat and other animals. It is of special interest to children.*

Season the flour and coat the rabbit joints.
Fry in the butter with the onions until brown.
Transfer to a pan with lentils, carrots, herbs,
and potatoes. Cover with the stock. Cook
gently until tender for about 1½ hours,
covered.

Add more stock if necessary with the tin of
drained sweetcorn. Remove the rabbit joints
to a warm serving dish. Sprinkle over the
chopped parsley.

*The historic town of Haverfordwest has a medieval quayside where new development has been skilfully blended with the old. Along the riverside, bustling with cafés, the wide pavements open on to **tea-gardens** and shops which although newly built add a Georgian feel to the façade.*

ROAST GROUSE WITH SAGE SAUCE

2 grouse, prepared
50g/2 oz butter
Pepper, freshly ground
Large bunch of fresh sage
25g/1 oz flour
50ml/2 fl oz red wine
Water

Wipe the grouse. Mix the butter and pepper together and rub all over the birds. Put them in a roasting pan and cook for 20 minutes at 220C/425F/Gas mark 7.

*Micro tip:
To use up every last drop of honey, put the jar in the microwave (without the lid) and heat on FULL for 20 seconds. The last of the honey will then pour out.

Remove and keep hot on a serving dish while making the sauce. Blend the flour with the juices in the roasting pan and pour in the wine. Put in the sage and simmer for 15 minutes, thinning if necessary with as much water as is needed to make a gravy consistency.

STEAK AND KIDNEY PIE

450g/1 lb lean stewing steak, cubed
100g/4 oz kidneys, cleaned and chopped
2 onions, sliced
175g/6 oz puff pastry
25g/1 oz butter
25g/1 oz flour plus 2 teaspoons
Salt and pepper
1 egg, beaten

Season 2 teaspoons of flour with the salt and pepper and toss the meat into it. Heat half the butter and fry the meat over a high heat until brown, adding the onions. Remove, place in a casserole dish and keep hot.

Blend the remaining flour into the juices, cook until thickened and spoon over the meat. Cook in the oven for 1½ hours at 160C/325F/ Gas mark 3 until the meat is tender.

Roll out the puff pastry and line a pie dish. Spoon in the meat and gravy. Use the remaining pastry to top the pie with a lid. Brush with the beaten egg. Bake at 200C/ 400F/Gas mark 6 for 40 minutes until golden. Serve with spring vegetables, sprinkle with chopped fresh herbs and serve immediately.

In the late 19th century when whooping cough was a prevalent disease it was common to pass small children through a bramble bush as a curative. Once passed through the bush an offering of bread-and-butter was left under the arch in the belief that the disease would be left behind with the food.

*Wild **spinach** is a sprawling perennial also known as Sea Beet. It is found widespread and common by the sea. Use the young leaves raw in salad, or cook as for spinach.*

BEEF IN PORT WINE

450g/1 lb beef cut into 18mm³/₄ inch cubes
25g/1 oz butter
1 tablespoon double cream
15g/¹/₂ oz arrowroot powder
225g/8 oz button mushrooms, cleaned
¹/₄ bottle Port Wine
Salt and black pepper

*It was noted as far back as the 12th century that almost the whole population of Wales lived on sheep, oats and **dairy** produce. These same ingredients still play a large part in the Welsh diet today.*

Heat the butter in a pan until bubbling. Toss in the beef chunks and turn over a few times to coat them. Mix the arrowroot with a litte water to pouring consistency.

Put the Port wine in a thick pan, add the mushrooms and bring to the boil. Pour in the arrowroot mixture and simmer until the port clears and looks like red jelly. Pour over the meat.

*Brecon Welsh Mineral Water, Brecon Beacons natural **waters** are available at National Trust properties such as Powys Castle .*

SHERRY TRIFLE

1 small stale sponge cake,
1 large glass of sherry
450g/1 lb strawberries, cleaned
300ml/10 fl oz double cream
600ml/1 pint milk
2 eggs
25g/1 oz cornflour
$\frac{1}{2}$ teaspoon vanilla essence

Cut the cake into slices and fit into the
bottom of the serving dish. Halve the
strawberries and arrange them on top of the
sponge cake.

Soak the cake with the sherry. Add more
strawberries to the top of the sponge cake.

Make the custard: mix the cornflour and eggs
into a bowl with the sugar and vanilla
essence. Bring the milk to the boil and
quickly mix into the egg mixture.

Pour into the saucepan and whisking, cook
for three minutes until thickened. Remove
from the heat and stir until cool. Pour over
the strawberries, and allow to set for 15
minutes.

Whip the double cream to a firm consistency
and spread over the cold custard. Decorate
the edge with cream rosettes and fresh
strawberry halves.

BLACKCURRANT PUDDING

40g/1 ¹/₂ oz blackcurrant jam
50g/2 oz caster sugar
175g/6 oz flour
75g/3 oz suet
1 egg, beaten
100ml/3 ¹/₂ fl oz milk
Knob of butter

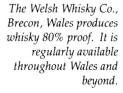

Mix the suet and flour together in a bowl and add the sugar. Mix in the egg and milk to a soft dough.

Grease a pudding basin with the butter and spoon in the jam. Put the dough in the basin and cover with greaseproof paper and foil over the top.

Steam for 1¹/₂ - 2 hours. Loosen the pudding with a knife and turn out. Serve with extra warmed jam if desired.

The Welsh Whisky Co., Brecon, Wales produces whisky 80% proof. It is regularly available throughout Wales and beyond.

MANDARIN RICE

100g/4 oz rice
600ml/1 pint milk
75g/3 oz caster sugar
100g/4 oz granulated sugar
1 vanilla pod
6 egg yolks
1½ tablespoons butter
450ml/ ½ pint water
450g/1 lb fresh mandarin oranges, peeled
2 tablespoons kirsch
½ tablespoon oil

Brush a mould with oil. Rinse the rice under running water and drain. Put into a saucepan with the milk, caster sugar, butter and vanilla pod and bring to the boil over a high heat until the sugar is dissolved. Place in an ovenproof dish and cook at 160C/325F/Gas mark 3 for 30 minutes.

Remove the vanilla pod. Lightly beat the egg yolks into the rice. Place in a mould and cool. Put the water and sugar into a saucepan and bring to the boil, stirring. Add half the oranges and heat for 10 minutes with strips of peel. Sieve. Return the sauce to the saucepan and cook over low heat until it thickens, stir in the kirsch. Leave until cool.

Turn the dessert on to a serving dish. Arrange the reserved mandarin oranges on the rice and pour over the sauce.

*Goats are to be seen frequently in Wales. It should be remembered that they are very partial to **blackcurrant** leaves and care should be taken to keep them away from these bushes at flowering time.*

***Samphire** is a fleshy green plant which grows on sea marshes and sand dunes in both South and West Wales. The green leaves are gathered in summer. Wash and boil for approximately 10 minutes until tender, toss in melted butter and serve as a vegetable to accompany meat dishes.*

QUAIL WITH SHERRY SAUCE

4 quail
300ml/¹/₂ pint stock
1 wineglass sherry
25g/1 oz butter
25g/1 oz flour

The commonest herb to use with lamb is rosemary but basil, bay, caraway, coriander, cumin, dill, hyssop, lemon balm, marjoram, mint, sage, savory, thyme are equally good and give a distinctive flavour.

Place the stock in a saucepan and simmer for ¹/₂ hour. Butter an ovenproof dish and lay in the quail. Roast in the oven at 190C/375F/Gas mark 5 for 25 - 30 minutes. Remove and keep hot.

Stir the flour into the juices in the pan, blend in the stock and sherry. Cook until the sauce has thickened and pour over the quail. Serve hot with buttered carrots and mange-tout.

SEAFOOD TERRINE

450g/1 lb white fish, filleted
225g/8 oz peeled prawns,
225g/8 oz scallops, cleaned
150ml/$^1/_4$ pint double cream
15g/$^1/_2$ oz butter
2 eggs
1 cup breadcrumbs
Salt and pepper
1 teaspoon cooking oil

*Heather, used at one time as a burning fuel for **baking** came from the drier slopes of Wales.*

Heat the butter in a pan, add the scallops and cook for 1 minute. Meanwhile, combine the fish, eggs, breadcrumbs, salt and pepper and cream in a processor.

Spread one-third of the blended mixture into an oiled mould, lay the scallops over the fish mixture. Top with a third of the fish. Cover this layer with prawns and finish with the remaining fish.

Place in a baking pan with hot water to come halfway up the sides of the dish and bake at 180C/350F/Gas mark 4 for 1 hour until set.

Allow to cool completely in a refrigerator then turn out, slice and garnish. Chopped chives could be added to the terrine for colour and flavour if desired. Serve with a tomato and basil salad (page 118).

The Welsh used to be known as 'seers' and as Celts many were able to tell fortunes by the tea leaves. After the user of the cup had drained off the last drops of liquid the user would swill round the cup three times anti-clockwise and turn it quickly upside down. The fortune was told by the shapes the leaves formed in the cup.

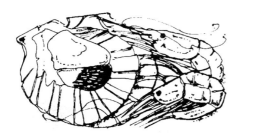

CHAPTER 5

The Festive Table

COUNTRY CHEESECAKES

Many charms involved the uses of onion and garlic. It was thought at one time that witches disliked onions intensely and to keep them in the house ensured protection against both witches and snakes.

225g/8 oz rich pastry
450g/1 lb curd cheese
25g/1 oz butter
100g/4 oz caster sugar
2 tablespoons cream
1 teaspoon grated nutmeg
75g/3 oz currants
3 eggs
$\frac{1}{4}$ cup brandy

Pre-heat the oven to 180C/350F/Gas mark 4. Line a 20cm/8 inch flan dish with the rolled out pastry. Rub the curd cheese through a sieve and beat in the butter, cream, sugar, nutmeg and currants.

*Micro tip:
To heat sardines in the microwave they should be arranged on a plate like the spokes of a wheel – the tails to the centre. Cook on FULL for 1 minute.

Blend the eggs and brandy into the mixture and spoon into the pastry case. Bake for 30 minutes.

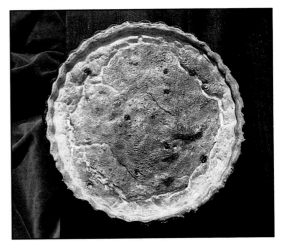

There are many areas of Wales today where people believe that keeping a hot cross bun – baked on Good Friday – imbues some magical healing power. The bun is wrapped tightly and stored away until the following year's bake. It is said that the bun never goes mouldy.

VEGETABLES BRAISED IN BEER

3 medium turnips, diced
3 large carrots, diced
2 large potatoes, chopped
2 leeks, sliced
1 large onion, sliced
25g/1 oz butter
300ml/$^1/_2$ pint beer
1 tablespoon tomato purée
1 tablespoon fresh thyme, chopped
Salt and Pepper

Melt the butter and add the sliced onions. Peel and dice the turnips, carrots and potatoes. Add to the onions. Cook for 5 minutes. Pour in the beer and bring to the boil.

Remove from the heat and add the salt, pepper, tomato purée, thyme and leeks. Place in a casserole and cook for 40 minutes.

To increase their beauty young girls have been told from time immemorial to drink an infusion of myrtle leaves.

65

CRAB SOUP

People from all over the world visit Wales for the Eisteddfod each year. Many an impromptu evening of singing, dancing and poetry is held around the farmhouse kitchens at this and other times for this is traditionally Welsh entertainment.

350g/12 oz crabmeat
50g/2 oz butter
2 carrots, peeled and chopped
1 small onion, peeled and chopped
$^1/_2$ cup white wine
2 tablespoons brandy
1 tablespoon tomato purée
450ml/$^3/_4$ pint fish stock
100ml/3$^1/_2$ fl oz fresh cream
Salt, pepper, cayenne
Thyme, parsley, coriander, chopped
Bay leaf

Cook the onion and carrots in the butter until soft but not browned. Moisten with the brandy which has been set alight. Allow the flames to subside and pour in the wine and stock. Add the thyme, bay leaf, parsley, coriander and season to taste. Allow to boil down gently by two-thirds. Remove the bay leaf and strain.

Purée the soup in a blender until fairly smooth. Stir in the crabmeat and tomato purée and cook gently for 15 minutes. Blend in the fresh cream.

The Griffin Inn at Llyswen is said to be the oldest sporting inn in Wales. A shooting and fishing school has been established at The Griffin to provide tuition to encourage newcomers to shooting - a sport that has provided pleasure for generations.

PHEASANT WITH PORT

2 pheasants
25g/1 oz butter
150ml/$\frac{1}{4}$ pint chicken stock
6 tablespoons port
1 orange, grated rind and juice
2 bay leaves
1 tablespoon cornflour
Salt and pepper
2 tablespoons water

Pre-heat the oven to 170C/325F/Gas mark 3.
Clean and wipe the pheasants. Season with
salt and pepper. Heat the butter in a casserole
and add the pheasants. Brown the birds all
over. Pour the stock and port over the birds.
Squeeze in the orange juice and add the finely
grated rind and bay leaf. Cover and cook in
the oven for 1 - 1$\frac{1}{2}$ hours.

Remove the birds from the casserole and
place on a warm dish. Mix the cornflour with
the water and stir into the liquid in the
casserole dish. Bring to the boil, stirring and
pour over the pheasants.

*Grouse feed on the young
shoots of heather and in
good seasons they are
proliferous in the hills
and moors of Wales. The
grouse shooting season
runs from August 12th -
December 10th when the
close season sets in.*

*In some parts of Wales it
is said that although
lamb is the traditional
Easter Sunday dinner
dish, no dogs should be
allowed to share this food
as they would go mad.*

APPLE STUFFED PARTRIDGE

2 partridges, cleaned and singed
1 tablespoon oil
1 onion, chopped
75g/3 oz finely minced beef
100g/4 oz apples
Salt and pepper
1 egg, beaten
1 tablespoon sage, finely chopped
450g/1 lb potatoes, cleaned
1 tablespoon brandy

There are some excellent British white wines – the best known being Croffta from Wales.

Fry the chopped onion in half the oil for 3 minutes. Add the minced beef and cook gently until the meat has turned colour.

According to legend, St. David was supposed to have lived for many years on bread and wild leeks. In honour of this, many Welshmen wear leeks rather than the traditional daffodil on March 1st – St. David's Day.

Peel and slice the apples and add to the pan. Stir in half the sage and brandy and cook until the apples are soft. Allow the mixture to cool and blend in the egg.

Stuff the partridges with the mixture. Transfer them to a roasting tin, brush with the remaining oil and sprinkle with the rest of the sage, salt and pepper. Cook for 35 minutes at 180C/350F/Gas mark 4 until browned.

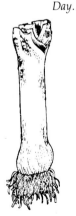

To make the game chips: peel and wash the potatoes well. Cut each potato into very thick rounds. Soak in cold water, dry on a towel and fry once in boiling fat for about 3 minutes. They need to be cooked but not brown. Drain.

Dust each chip with hot spices such as paprika pepper or cayenne for additional flavour. Serve with fresh carrots and peas.

STRAWBERRY CREAM

Apart from Welsh wines there are also Welsh beers and Welsh whisky.

396g/14 oz fresh strawberries
100g/4 fl oz light cream
1 packet strawberry jelly
1 egg

Simmer the strawberries gently in a saucepan for 5 minutes, reserving a few for decoration. Drain the fruit and place the juice in a pan with the jelly. Stir over heat until dissolved.

Liquidise the fruit in a blender and add to the jelly. Cool in the refrigerator until the jelly is on the point of setting.

Separate the egg. Whisk the yolk into the cream. Stir into the jelly and leave until almost set. Whisk the egg white and fold into the jelly.

Pour into tall glasses or a mould and leave to set. Decorate with whipped cream and the remaining strawberries.

*Micro tip:
If the sugar or salt gets damp, heat in the microwave for 30 seconds, depending on the amount. Be sure to remove any metal lids if it has been stored in a jar.

MINCE PIES

225g/8 oz flour
175g/6 oz butter
225g/8 oz mincemeat
1 teaspoon lemon juice
Water

Sieve the flour on to a clean surface, make a well in the centre and put in the lemon juice and a little water. Blend in the edges of the flour until a thick paste is formed.

Knead until smooth, roll out to a rectangle and place the butter on one half of the pastry. Fold over the other half of the pastry to enclose the butter. Press the edges together with the rolling pin and roll out to about three times the original length. Fold the pastry into three, lengthwise.

Chill for 30 minutes, roll out and fold again. Repeat this procedure 5 times keeping the pastry in the lengthwise shape with each rolling out. Chill for a further 30 minutes before using.

Roll out and line some patty-tins. Fill with mincemeat. Cover with pastry lids and brush over lightly with water and dredge with sugar. Bake at 220C/425F/Gas mark 7 for 20 minutes.

The old physicians in Wales have been known to have practised the ancient art of healing since the 13th century using common, everyday herbs, plants and wisdom. Some herbs were believed to be endowed with magical virtues while others were administered to prevent fevers or to cure the 'rheumatics'. The use of water from certain wells was thought to be an essential ingredient of the medicine. Many of these medicines are still in use today.

The river Dee is known world wide as a salmon river.

MULLED WINE

600ml/1 pint port
300ml/$^{1}/_{2}$ pint water
75g/3 oz sugar
$^{1}/_{2}$ teaspoon cinnamon
$^{1}/_{2}$ teaspoon ginger
8 cloves
1 lemon, grated rind and juice
Slices of orange

Mix together the water, sugar, cinnamon, ginger and lemon and boil in a large saucepan. Add the port and heat but do not allow to boil. Serve hot with the orange slices studded with the cloves floating on the top.

Fishing is available at Nantymoch and Dinas reservoirs.

RICH CHRISTMAS PUDDING

100g/4 oz shredded suet
100g/4 oz raisins
100g/4 oz sultanas
100g/4 oz breadcrumbs
50g/2 oz currants
50g/2 oz flour
50g/2 oz mixed peel
50g/2 oz chopped nuts
75g/3 oz sugar
15g/$^{1}/_{2}$ oz mixed spice
15g/$^{1}/_{2}$ oz cinnamon
15g/$^{1}/_{2}$ oz nutmeg
Juice and rind of 1 lemon
2 eggs
1 wineglass of brandy
1 wineglass of rum

Llanybydder is a market town noted for its monthly horse sales as well as for its traditional wholesome produce.

Mix all the dry ingredients together, stir in the well-beaten eggs, brandy and rum. Turn into a well-greased basin and steam for 6 - 7 hours.

72

SNOWCAPPED MOUNTAIN DEW

75g/3 oz chopped nuts
100g/4 oz sugar
450ml/³/₄ pint double cream, whipped
150ml/¹/₄ pint water
2 wine glasses Cân-y-Delyn liqueur

Put the sugar and water into a thick pan and boil quickly until the mixture resembles a pale toffee colour.

Remove the pan from the heat and add the crushed walnuts, stirring all the time until cold. Add the whipped cream and stir in the liqueur. Whip again and serve chilled, topped with a walnut.

*Micro tip:
To remove peach skins easily, heat whole peaches in the microwave for 30 seconds. Leave to stand for 5 minutes then peel away the skins.

Many farmers believed that to carry a freshly dug potato around in the pocket until it had turned quite black and hard was a cure for rheumatism.

CHAPTER 6

The Winter Table

PLUM PIE

*Micro tip:
Shells make an
attractive container for
fish dishes. (See
Seafood Shells on page
110). They are
microwave safe and
dishwasher proof and
a dish looks attractive
when served on a
plain plate.

225g/8 oz self raising flour
3 tablespoons caster sugar
Pinch of salt
100g/4 oz butter
675g/1 $\frac{1}{2}$ lb fresh plums
2 tablespoons ground rice
1 egg, beaten
1 beaten egg white

Rub the butter into the flour and stir in the
sugar, salt and beaten egg. Mix to a dough
and chill for 30 minutes. Roll out the dough
and line a deep pie dish.

Halve and stone the plums. Poach with one
tablespoon of the sugar until cooked. Drain.
Arrange the plums in the pie dish. Sprinkle
over the ground rice and one tablespoon of
sugar. Cover with the rest of the pastry and
brush the surface with the egg white and
remaining sugar. Bake at 190C/375F/Gas
mark 5 for 40 minutes. Serve hot or cold.

*It is an established belief
along the Welsh border
that if a hen comes into
the house then a visitor
will follow shortly
afterwards.*

74

MUFFINS

1.5 kg/3 lb flour
1 tablespoon salt
25g/1 oz fresh yeast
$\frac{1}{2}$ tablespoon sugar
600ml/1 pint warm water
2 tablespoons fine semolina

Sift the flour and salt together. Cream the yeast
with the sugar and a little of the warm water.
Mix into the flour with as much water as is
necessary to form a stiff dough. Knead well
and leave to rise until double in size.

Knead again and divide the dough into pieces
roughly 50g/2 oz each. Shape into rounds with
a cutter, on a floured surface, to prevent them
sticking. Bake on a greased griddle over gentle
heat, for two minutes on each side. Dust with
fine semolina and serve sliced and toasted with
butter.

*Look out for the country **produce** available from the bustling street markets popular in Wales; succulent shellfish fresh-caught by local fishermen, tender lamb and the freshest of vegetables, herbs and farmhouse cheeses are always available.*

It is regarded as lucky if the first lamb to be seen in the spring is a black one.

75

*Micro tip:
*Mange-tout are also
known as snow peas.
Add 1 tablespoon water
to snow peas in a shallow
dish, cover, cook on full
for 3 minutes and they
are ready to serve.*

FARMHOUSE LOAF

225g/8 oz lean minced beef
225g/8 oz minced pork
100g/4 oz breadcrumbs
1 teaspoon mustard
1 tablespoon, chopped mixed herbs
1 large onion, finely chopped
1 tablespoon cooking oil
1 clove garlic, crushed
1 egg

Blend the meat with the garlic, breadcrumbs
and onion. Mix in the egg, mustard and the
herbs and mould into a round shape.

Put the oil in a baking tray and add the loaf.
Bake at 190C/375F/Gas mark 5 for 40
minutes. Remove the meat from the pan,
slice and serve with a rich gravy.

*Micro tip:
Whole **Asparagus**
spears should be
arranged on a plate
like the spokes of a
wheel with the heads
facing inwards and
microwaved for 1
minute on FULL.

76

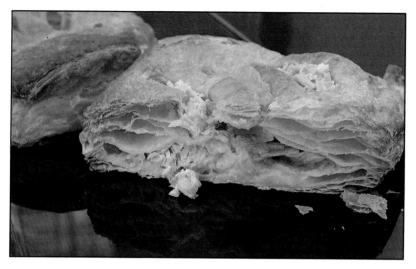

SALMON IN PASTRY

225g/8 oz puff pastry
175g/6 oz cooked, fresh salmon
2 leeks, cleaned, chopped and cooked
15g/$^1/_2$ oz flour
15g/$^1/_2$ oz butter
150ml/$^1/_2$ pint milk
Salt and pepper

*Farmers used to grow
parsley in large
quantities to feed to their
sheep. Parsley was once
thought to be an
antidote to poison and
has been used for
centuries to cure some
illnesses in adults.*

Melt the butter in a saucepan and stir in the
flour. Cook for 1 minute and gradually blend
in the milk. Cook to a thick sauce and season
with the salt and pepper.

Roll out the pastry and cut into squares. Lay
a piece of cooked salmon in the centre of each
square. Cover with the well-drained leeks
and the sauce. Cut another square of pastry.
Lay over the leeks and seal the edges.

Twist one corner and cut a decoration into the
pastry. Glaze with the egg and cook at
200C/400F/Gas mark 6 for 30 minutes.

WARM LEMON TART

*Micro tip:

If you do not have a 300ml/½ pint **measuring jug** use a large tea-cup or mug. It measures approximately ½ pint and can be placed directly in the microwave for heating liquids, providing it does not have any metallic decoration on it.

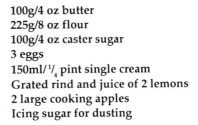

100g/4 oz butter
225g/8 oz flour
100g/4 oz caster sugar
3 eggs
150ml/¼ pint single cream
Grated rind and juice of 2 lemons
2 large cooking apples
Icing sugar for dusting

Rub the butter into the flour until the mixture resembles breadcrumbs. Stir in 1 tablespoon of the caster sugar. Bind to a dough with 4 tablespoons of water.

Roll out the pastry and line a greased flan tin. Chill in the refrigerator for 30 minutes.

Pre-heat the oven to 200C/400F/Gas mark 6. Prick the pastry all over with a fork and line with greaseproof paper and baking beans. Bake for 15 minutes but do not allow to brown.

Reduce the heat to 180C/350F/Gas mark 4. Remove the beans and paper and replace in the oven for a further 5 minutes.

Beat the eggs, cream and the rest of the sugar together. Whisk in the rind and juice of the lemons. Peel, core and coarsely grate the apples. Add to the lemon mixture and fill the pastry case.

According to a nineteenth century myth warts could be made to vanish by rubbing them with the blood of an eel.

Bake for 35 - 40 minutes. Dust with icing sugar and serve warm.

*Micro tip:
To add volume when whisking egg whites, microwave on HIGH for 5 - 8 seconds and beat the whites quickly with a pinch of salt.

OATMEAL AND ONION LOAF

175g/6 oz flour
100g/4 oz oatmeal
150ml/5 fl oz milk
1 teaspoon baking powder
Salt and pepper
1 tablespoon oil
2 large onions, peeled and finely chopped
2 tablespoons chopped parsley
Milk to glaze
Greased baking sheet

Pre-heat the oven to 230C/450F/Gas mark 8. Soak the oatmeal in the milk.

In a separate bowl mix together the flour, baking powder, salt and pepper. Stir in the oil, chopped onions and parsley.

Add the oatmeal and a little more milk, if necessary, and knead for 3 - 4 minutes.

Halve the dough and roll each piece into an oblong shape, about 30cm/12 inches long. Cross the pieces over each other to form a twist. Pinch the ends together.

The largest herb garden in Mid Wales is to be seen in the seven-acre gardens of Plas Penhelig Country House Hotel. The hotel also boasts a walled kitchen garden which supplies the hotel with almost all of its fresh vegetables throughout the year.

Place on a baking sheet and brush with milk. Sprinkle with a little extra oatmeal if desired. Bake for about 25 minutes.

Eat hot or cold with a filling farmhouse soup.

FISHERMAN'S PIE

450g/1 lb white fish, filleted
450ml/$^3/_4$ pint milk
1 bay leaf
1 small onion, chopped
25g/1 oz flour
25g/1 oz butter
100g/4 oz grated cheese
Salt and pepper
450g/1 lb potatoes, mashed
$^1/_4$ teaspoon cayenne pepper

*Micro tip:
Cook pastry cases for
such dishes as lemon
meringue pie unfilled.
Use a mixture of plain
and wholemeal flour
for colour and prick
the base of the pastry
case very thoroughly
with a fork to ensure
even cooking.

In an ovenproof dish place the fish, milk, bay
leaf and onion. Season. Cover and bake at
180C/350F/Gas mark 4 for 25 minutes.

Remove the fish and flake using a fork into an
ovenproof dish. Melt the butter in a pan and
stir in the flour. Add the milk from the fish
and cook gently for 2 minutes. Remove the
bay leaf and stir in three-quarters of the
grated cheese. Spread the mashed potatoes
over the fish.

Sprinkle with the rest of the cheese and the
cayenne and bake at 200C/400F/Gas mark 6
for 15 minutes until browned on the top.

PEAR DESSERT

*Micro tip:
Seasoning tends to
have a toughening
effect and it is wise to
add the minimum
when cooking in the
microwave, especially
on poultry and other
meat. Adjust the
seasoning at the end of
the cooking period.

Large can pear halves, drained
100g/4 oz self raising flour
75g/3 oz castor sugar
3 eggs, beaten
$\frac{1}{2}$ pint milk
1 teaspoon vanilla essence
$\frac{1}{2}$ teaspoon butter
1 tablespoon icing sugar

Grease a baking dish with the butter and
place the drained pears in the dish. Combine
the flour and sugar in a basin and stir in the
eggs, milk and vanilla essence. Beat to a
smooth batter.

Pour the batter mixture over the fruit and
bake in a moderate oven for about 45 minutes
until the top is brown and crispy.

Allow to cool a little and sprinkle over the
icing sugar. Serve with fresh cream or a
scoopful of ice-cream if desired.

82

Lobster pots can be seen on the quayside at the small fishing port of New Quay, where local boats sell their freshly-caught fish almost daily. It is of particular interest to the summer visitor and to keen anglers.

MUSHROOM CHOP

4 pork chops
225g/8 oz leeks, cleaned and chopped
450g/l lb new potatoes, peeled
225g/8 oz carrots, peeled and sliced
100g/4 oz mushrooms
25g/1 oz flour
25g/1 oz butter
300ml/$^1/_2$ pint milk
Salt

Fry the pork chops in a little of the butter until tender. Boil the potatoes and carrots for 20 minutes, drain and keep hot. Cook the leeks in boiling, salted water, drain and keep hot.

A superstition amongst poultry keepers states that it is unlucky to burn an empty egg-shell. To do so would herald an omen that all the birds would at once cease to lay.

Transfer the chops onto a warmed dish and make the mushroom sauce by putting the rest of the butter into the frying pan. Quickly cook the mushrooms until just tender. Stir in the flour and cook for 1 minute. Blend in the milk stirring all the time until the sauce thickens. Arrange the vegetables and chops on each plate and spoon over the sauce.

CHAPTER 7
The Vegetarian Table

APPLE BROWN BETTY

675g/1½ lb cooking apples, peeled and cored
175g/6 oz fresh brown breadcrumbs
Juice and grated rind of 1 lemon

*Micro tip:
Cooked jacket potatoes
will keep warm for up
to 2 hours if they are
wrapped in foil the
minute they come out
of the oven.

75g/3 oz brown sugar
2 tablespoons honey
1 tablespoon water
2 teaspoons butter

Grease an ovenproof dish with half the butter.
Sprinkle some of the breadcrumbs into the
bottom and sides of the dish. Slice the apples
and layer half into the dish. Top with a layer
of crumbs and the remaining apples.

Put the rind and juice of the lemon into a
saucepan with the sugar, water and honey
and heat. Pour over the apples and cover
with the remaining breadcrumbs.

Dot with the butter and bake at 180C/350F/
Gas mark 4 for 1 hour until the apples are
tender and the pudding is brown.

*Many of the Welsh
farmers lead the way in
organic farming,
Brynllys Organic farm
being one of the most
well-known.*

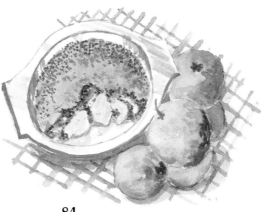

*Almost any home-grown **produce** can be bought from the roadside stalls, common in Wales, including honey, sausages, ice cream and farmhouse cheeses.*

ONION CAKE

675g/1½ lb thinly sliced potatoes
2 large finely chopped onions
50g/2 oz melted butter
2 tomatoes
Salt and pepper

Grease a cake tin or an ovenproof dish and place a layer of potato in the base. Season with salt and pepper and sprinkle with a layer of chopped onion.

Add a further layer of potato and brush with melted butter. Season and continue, finishing with a layer of potato.

Brush the top with butter and bake for 40 minutes at 190C/375F/Gas mark 5.

Finely slice the tomatoes and place on the top of the cake. Return to the oven and cook for a further 10 minutes.

Stone Hall Hotel and Restaurant, Welsh Hook , is situated just off the main A40 Haverfordwest to Fishguard road and is famous for its quail roasts, local scallops and pan-fried salmon.

85

STILTON & CELERY SOUP

1 head of celery, chopped
1 onion, chopped
50g/2 oz butter
50g/2 oz flour
600ml/1 pint chicken stock
100g/4 oz blue Stilton cheese
2 tablespoons brandy
Salt and pepper

*Set **yoghurt** made with sheep's milk is easily obtained in Wales and can be used when making a whortleberry tart.*

Cook celery and onion in the butter until soft but not brown. Reduce the heat and stir in the flour. Gradually add the stock, stirring all the time. Bring to the boil, reduce the heat and simmer for 30 minutes.

Season the soup and blend in a liquidiser until smooth. Return the soup to a saucepan and reheat over a low heat.

Crumble the Stilton and add it to the soup, then stir in the brandy. Pour into individual bowls and serve.

*Micro tip:
Milk for cereals may be heated in the serving bowl. This is especially useful for quick porridge.

SAVOURY BISCUITS

100g/4 oz flour
50g/2 oz butter
1 egg plus 1 yolk
Milk
$\frac{1}{2}$ teaspoon cayenne pepper
Fat for greasing
Sea salt

Rub the butter into the flour until it resembles breadcrumbs. Stir in the cayenne pepper.

Beat the egg with a little milk and pour into the flour. Mix well and knead for a few minutes. Chill in the refrigerator for about 1 hour. Roll out very thinly and cut into biscuits with a cookie cutter. Pierce with a fork and brush with the egg yolk. Sprinkle with the sea salt.

Grease a baking tray and bake for about 6 minutes at 200C/400F/Gas mark 6.

*A **sturgeon** weighing 176 kg and 2.75 m in length was caught on the River Teifi in 1932. Inside the fish were enough sprats to fill two buckets.*

In May, each year, a leek-throwing competition is held in the village of Crickhowell situated near the limestone summit known as Table Mountain.

87

*Micro tip:
Fresh **fish** cooks in the microwave beautifully. Brush with milk, season lightly, place in a shallow dish and put several small pieces of butter on the surface of the fish. Cover with cling film. Look up timings for different variations in your microwave cookery book.

RHUBARB CRUMBLE

450g/1 lb rhubarb, cleaned and cut into chunks
100g/4 oz flour
50g/2 oz sugar
100g/4 oz soft brown sugar
$\frac{1}{2}$ teaspoon nutmeg
$\frac{1}{2}$ teaspoon cinnamon
50g/2 oz butter plus 1 teaspoon
2 tablespoons water

Grease a pie dish. Put the rhubarb into the pie dish. Add the water and sprinkle with half the sugar.

To find out more about Welsh hill farming go and see Trefrifawr Farm trail, Tywyn, overlooking the Dyfi estuary. There is also the Holgates Honey Farm in the same vicinity on the outskirts of Tywyn.

Make the crumble by sifting the flour into a bowl. Rub in the butter until the mixture resembles breadcrumbs. Stir in the spices and brown sugar and spoon over the fruit.

Bake at 180C/350F/Gas mark 4 for 40 minutes. Serve hot with custard.

CAULIFLOWER CHEESE FLAN

150g/5 oz flour
$\frac{1}{2}$ teaspoon salt
75g/3 oz butter plus 1 teaspoon
1 egg yolk
100g/4 oz cooked cauliflower
100g/4 oz Caerphilly cheese
2 eggs, separated
300ml/$\frac{1}{2}$ pint milk
Salt and pepper

Rub the butter into the flour until the mixture
resembles breadcrumbs. Add the salt and
egg yolk and mix with a little water until a
stiff dough is formed. Roll out. Grease and
line a flan tin or a 23cm/9 inch tart dish.

Lay the cauliflower in the bottom of the flan
dish. Crumble over the Caerphilly cheese
and season to taste. Beat the egg yolks into
the milk. Whisk the whites until stiff and fold
into the egg and milk.

Pour into the flan case and bake at 200C/
400F/Gas mark 6 for 40 minutes.

*Micro tip:
For a quick **orange
icing** – grate the rind
of an orange into a
small bowl. Add the
squeezed juice and
heat on HIGH for 1
minute. Beat in sifted
icing sugar to the
required stiffness.

*Stilton and Guinness
Pâté is a delicacy of
Wales.*

BAKED TURNIPS

675g/1¹/₂ lb young turnips
25g/1 oz butter
300ml/¹/₂ pint milk
Salt and pepper
1 clove garlic
25g/1 oz breadcrumbs
Chopped parsley

Peel and part boil the turnips for about 10
minutes. Drain well, allow to cool and cut
into slices. Butter a pie dish and arrange the
sliced turnips in the dish. Crush the garlic
over the turnips and gently pour in the milk.

Season with salt and pepper. Cover with the
breadcrumbs and bake for 30 minutes at
180C/350F/Gas mark 4 until the top is
brown.

Sprinkle with chopped parsley and serve
with Vegetables in Beer (see page 65).

*Micro tip:
Herbs can be dried for
future use. Microwave
on HIGH until dry.
Store in glass
containers with sealed
lids.

BUBBLE AND SQUEAK

2 onions, finely chopped
75g/3 oz butter
175g/6 oz mashed potatoes
450g/1 lb cooked brussels sprouts, shredded
Nutmeg

Cook the onion in half the butter. Mix the
potatoes, brussels and onion together. Season
with the nutmeg.

Shape into little flat cakes and fry in the
remaining butter until brown on both sides.
Serve with Baked Turnips (above) and
Vegetables in Beer (see page 65).

*There are many
Women's Institute Co-
operative markets held
throughout Wales where
some of the best freshly
cooked farmhouse
produce is regularly
available at reasonable
cost.*

MACKEREL WITH GOOSEBERRY SAUCE

*Micro tip:
Put **Corn on the cob**
into microwave boiling
bags and cook two
cobs for 9 minutes on
FULL. No water is
required and they will
keep hot for 10
minutes if the bag is
not opened.

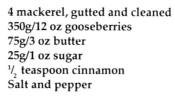

4 mackerel, gutted and cleaned
350g/12 oz gooseberries
75g/3 oz butter
25g/1 oz sugar
$\frac{1}{2}$ teaspoon cinnamon
Salt and pepper

Top and tail the gooseberries and cook in 2
tablespoons of water until soft but not
broken. Put three-quarters of the fruit
through a sieve. Beat half the butter into the
sieved sauce and add the sugar and a pinch of
cinnamon, salt and pepper. Add the rest of
the cooked fruit to the sauce.

Place the cleaned fish in a buttered ovenproof
dish. Season with salt and pepper and dot
with butter. Cover with foil and bake in the
oven at 180C/350F/Gas mark 4 for 20
minutes.

Remove from the oven. Split each mackerel
in half lengthwise and remove the backbone.
Serve hot with the gooseberry sauce, fresh
new potatoes and summer vegetables.

*There is a **picnic** area at
Buttington Wharf, to the
north of Welshpool,
Montgomeryshire, with
plenty to see and do in
the area.*

LIGHT FRUIT CAKE

*Although the rhododendron plant was introduced into Britain from the Mediterranean in 1763 as an ornamental bush and as pheasant cover on larger estates, it grows abundantly in Wales and the West Country, is poisonous to **livestock** and prevents the growith of other plants.*

225g/8 oz self-raising flour
225g/8 oz mixed fruit
50g/2 oz mixed peel
100g/4 oz butter
100g/4 oz sugar
2 eggs, beaten
1 teaspoon baking powder
1 teaspoon mixed spice
50ml/2 fl oz milk

Mix the flour with the sugar, peel and dried fruit. Stir in the eggs and butter. Add the milk and spices and beat together until thoroughly mixed.

*Why not pay a visit to Erddig? This grand late 17th century, National Trust property is situated near Wrexham, Clwyd and includes many old artefacts in the **kitchen**, laundry and bakehouse.*

Turn into a greased cake tin and bake for $1^{1}/_{2}$ hours at 180C/350F/Gas mark 4 until browned. Test with a skewer to ensure the centre of the cake is cooked. Allow to cool for 10 minutes in the tin then turn out.

CHAPTER 8

The Outdoor Table

POTTED PRAWNS

At one time Aberaeron was a fishing port. Nowadays it is a popular haven for summer visitors as well as fishermen.

225gm/8 oz peeled prawns
A few whole prawns to garnish
75g/3 oz butter
2 teaspoons lemon juice
Slices of lemon to garnish
4 teaspoons chopped parsley
Cayenne pepper

Finely chop the prawns. Soften the butter. Beat the prawns into half the butter with the lemon juice and parsley. Turn into individual serving dishes and smooth over the tops.

Melt the remaining butter and pour over the pâté. Sprinkle a little cayenne over the butter and chill in the refrigerator for at least an hour. Garnish with whole prawns and lemon slices and serve with chunks of fresh bread or Cheese Shortbreads (see page 97).

*There is a tradition that the **leek** became a national emblem of Wales when used at the battle of Meigen in the seventh century; some say that King Arthur won a victory over Saxon invaders by Welsh troops wearing leeks in their caps thus distinguishing themselves from the opposition.*

*It was not so long ago that many people in Wales would consult a wizard if their **cattle** were ailing. A wizard was said to have had the 'second sight'– a gift only given to great men.*

FAIRY CAKES

100g/4 oz margarine
100g/4 oz self-raising flour
1 large egg, beaten
100g/4 oz caster sugar
2 teaspoons baking powder
2 tablespoons boiling water
50g/2 oz currants

Cream the margarine and sugar together until light in colour. Stir in the beaten egg and gradually blend in the flour.

Add as much hot water as is necessary to form a heavy consistency. Stir in the baking powder and currants.

Grease a bun tray. Bake for 8 - 10 minutes at 200C/400F/Gas mark 6 until golden. Dust with icing sugar.

*Up until a few years ago the country people of Wales considered it improper to buy their **meat** in the town and always insisted on making their purchases from market stalls, so prolific are the markets in Welsh towns.*

95

BANANA & NUT TEABREAD

400g/14 oz self-raising flour
100g/4 oz caster sugar
100g/4 oz butter plus 1 teaspoon
50g/2 oz nuts, chopped
2 teaspoons baking powder
3 eggs, beaten
4 ripe bananas
$\frac{1}{2}$ teaspoon vanilla essence

Pre-heat the oven to 180C/350F/Gas mark 4 and grease a loaf tin. Cream the butter and sugar together and beat until light in colour. Add the eggs. Mash the bananas and stir into the mixture. Beat well. Blend in the flour, nuts, baking powder and vanilla essence.

Pour the mixture into the loaf tin and bake for 45 minutes until firm to the touch. Turn on to a rack to cool. This tea-bread is best wrapped in foil and kept for 1 - 2 days before eating. Slice and butter.

Some of the excellent Welsh **breads** come from local bakeries. Traditional baked products such as Bara Brith (fruit loaf) and Welshcakes (traditional Welsh scones) are easily available, but look out for Plum bread and Floury Batch – a long thinnish loaf, covered in flour which looks like a very long bread roll.

CHEESE SHORTBREADS

225g/8 oz flour
225g/8 oz butter plus 1 teaspoon
225g/8 oz cheese, crumbled
Salt and pepper
1 teaspoon nutmeg

Rub the butter into the flour until it resembles breadcrumbs. Stir in the salt, pepper and nutmeg. Mix in the crumbled cheese. Knead to a firm dough and place in the refrigerator to cool for 10 minutes.

Lightly grease two baking sheets with the remaining butter. Roll out the shortbread mixture and cut into rounds or required shapes. Lay on the baking sheet and mark with a criss-cross pattern on the top of each one.

*Micro tip:
Bread rolls can be warmed by putting them in a bread basket in a napkin and microwave on FULL for 30 seconds.

Bake in a pre-heated oven at 190C/375F/Gas mark 5 for 15 - 20 minutes. Leave to cool on the tray before removing to a wire rack.

POACHER'S PASTIES

225g/8 oz flour plus 1 tablespoon
100g/4 oz rabbit meat, minced
100g/4 oz pheasant meat, chopped
4 tablespoon cooking oil
1 onion, cleaned and chopped
1 large potato, chopped
Salt and pepper
50g/2 oz mushrooms, cleaned and chopped
2 teaspoons fresh thyme
100ml/3$\frac{1}{2}$ fl oz chicken stock
2 egg yolks, beaten
75g/3 oz butter
Water

St. Monacella is the patron saint of hares. There is a fifteenth-century church that houses the shrine to St. Monacella and stands on the banks of the upper stretches of the Tanat at Pennant Melangell's.

Rub the butter into the flour until it resembles crumbs. Mix in three-quarters of the beaten eggs and as much water as is needed to form a soft dough. Refrigerate until cold.

Coat the rabbit and pheasant with the tablespoon of flour. Heat half the oil in a frying pan and cook the meat and thyme for 5 minutes. Add the leeks and mushrooms and continue cooking for a further 5 minutes. Stir in the chicken stock. Season with the salt and pepper and cook for a further 15 minutes.

*The Sand **Leek** is a relative of garlic and can be found under hedges, on banks and in rough pastures. Stems and bulbs can be used in the same way as garlic.*

Roll out the pastry and cut into rounds the size of saucers. Place a little of the meat and mushroom mixture in the centre. Brush the sides of the pastry with water and fold over.

Crimp the edges together and pierce each pasty on the top. Brush with the remainder of the beaten egg. Bake at 190C/375F/Gas mark 5 for 20 minutes until the pastry is browned. Serve cold with a green salad.

The Montgomeryshire Canal is a wonderful place for wildlife and almost 30 miles of the towpath can be walked along. Many fishing matches are held along the banks and the canal is regularly re-stocked with fish.

PICNIC TARTS

175g/6 oz flour
100g/4 oz butter plus 1 teaspoon
$\frac{1}{2}$ teaspoon salt
$\frac{1}{2}$ teaspoon cayenne pepper
Water
3 eggs plus 1 egg yolk
4 rashers of bacon
1 onion

Put the flour and salt into a basin and rub in the butter until the mixture resembles breadcrumbs. Add the egg yolk and mix to a stiff dough with the water.

Roll out and line a greased tartlet tin. Line with greaseproof paper and fill with baking beans. Bake blind at 180C/350F/Gas mark 4 for 15 minutes. Remove the greaseproof paper and beans, replace in the oven for a further 5 minutes.

Clean and chop the onion and chop the bacon. Lay in the bottom of each pastry case. Mix together the beaten eggs and season with salt and cayenne pepper. Pour on top of the onion and bacon.

*Micro Tip:
Place the rindless bacon on a plate. Cover with a sheet of kitchen paper. Place in a microwave oven and heat on high for two minutes. Crumble when cool.

Bake in the oven for 15 - 20 minutes until golden on the top. Remove the tarts from the tin and allow to cool completely before wrapping carefully.

SMOKED SALMON SPREAD

100g/4 oz smoked salmon pieces
$^1/_2$ glass dry sherry
150ml/$^1/_4$ pint cream
100g/4oz fresh white breadcrumbs
300ml/$^1/_2$ pint thick béchamel sauce
1 dessertspoon anchovy essence

Mince the smoked salmon and stir into the
béchamel sauce with the breadcrumbs. Pour
in the sherry and beat with the cream and
anchovy essence.

Turn into small individual dishes and garnish
with sliced gherkin and a sprig of fresh fennel
if available. Makes the ideal sandwich filler
or can be spread on crackers or toast.

*Caerphilly, a delightful
cheese, is named after the
town of that name in
South Wales. Somehow
it tastes better eaten in a
field with an apple and a
hunk of fresh bread. Try
it!*

*The Moors Farm
Collection of rare breeds
of animals with many
varieties of wildfowl,
pheasants and poultry is
situated one mile north of
Welshpool in
Montgomeryshire.*

BARA BRITH

* Micro tip:
When cooking liver or
kidneys pierce the
thin outer membrane
with a fork or knife.
Prick each piece
evenly all over. This
prevents them from
exploding in the
cooker.

450g/1 lb flour
300ml/¹/₂ pint cold tea
225g/8 oz dried mixed fruit
100g/4 oz soft brown sugar
1 teaspoon nutmeg
Fat for greasing
1 egg
1 tablespoon milk

Soak the dried fruit in tea overnight. Put the
flour, sugar and nutmeg into a bowl. Beat the
egg and mix into the flour adding the fruit
and as much liquid as is necessary to form a
stiff dough.

Line a small loaf tin with buttered paper.
Turn the mixture into the tin and bake at
150C/300F/Gas mark 2 for 1¹/₂ hours. Cool
and remove from the tin. Store for at least 2
days, well-wrapped. Slice and butter.

*The town of Welshpool,
Montgomeryshire, was
granted a market charter
in 1263 from
Gwenwynwyn, Prince of
Powys.*

102

At the turn of the century Cardigan Bay was known to be full of shoals of herring and mackerel.

QUEEN CAKES

175g/6 oz flour
100g/4 oz butter
100g/4 oz currants
100g/4 oz caster sugar
2 eggs, beaten
1 teaspoon baking powder
1 teaspoon lemon juice
1 tablespoon milk
50ml/2 fl oz double cream

Place 18 paper cases in bun tins and heat the oven to 190C/375F/Gas mark 5. Cream the butter and sugar together until thick and light in colour. Add the cream and lemon juice and beat until well mixed.

Blend in the eggs, flour and baking powder, adding the milk if necessary. Stir in the currants. Beat well and spoon into the paper cases. Bake for 15 minutes until golden brown.

*Micro tip:
Biscuits, crackers and peanuts that have gone soft can be resurrected if they are placed on absorbent paper and microwaved on FULL for 35 seconds.

103

CHAPTER 9

The Occasional Table

POOR MAN'S BRUNCH

Allow 3 slices of thick sliced white bread per
person
3 egg yolks
1 cup milk
3 tablespoons butter
3 tablespoons caster sugar
$\frac{1}{2}$ teaspoon vanilla extract
Cinnamon

*Cockle gathering is older
than mining and at one
time cockle gatherers
consisted of mostly
women, young and old.
Nearly everyone rode a
donkey and carried great
baskets ready for the sea
harvesting of cockles in
the summer and mussels
in the winter. The shell-
fish lie an inch below the
sand and once collected
can be boiled, pickled or
fried in butter, generally
served with chopped leeks
and bacon.*

Remove the crusts from the bread. Bring the
milk to the boil with one tablespoon of sugar
and the vanilla extract. Pour the milk into a
soup plate. Cool a little and quickly dip each
slice of bread in it and lay them on a plate to
drain.

Beat up the yolks of the eggs. Lay each slice
of bread into the egg mixture, quickly, on
both sides, using a spatula. Put the slices to
drain on a clean cloth and melt the butter in a
frying pan. When the butter starts to smoke
fry the slices and brown on both sides.

Remove the bread from the pan and sprinkle
the browned slices with sugar and cinnamon.

Cut each bread slice in half. Serve piled up
and wrapped in a clean napkin to keep warm
while you are frying the rest of the slices.

TEISEN PLANC

350g/12 oz sweetened shortcrust pastry
175g/6 oz raspberry jam
Caster sugar

Roll out the pastry, 5 mm/$\frac{1}{4}$ inch thick, and
cut into two rounds, the size of a dinner plate.
Spread one piece of pastry with the jam.
Raspberry is traditional but any flavoured
jam can be used. Place the other round of
pastry on top of the jam and seal the edges.

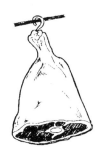

Carefully transfer to a griddle and bake until
golden brown, about 8 minutes. Turn and
bake on the other side. Sprinkle with caster
sugar and serve hot.

*As late as the 1980's
hams could be seen
hanging from large hooks
in the ceiling in many
country farmhouses,
although it is fast
becoming a nostalgic
memory.*

*Micro tip:
Oven bags are good to
use in the microwave
but be careful of a
sudden burst of steam
when opening the bag.

ASPARAGUS WITH SALMON & YOGHURT DIP

175g/6 oz fresh cooked salmon, flaked
300ml/¹/₂ pint yoghurt
2 tablespoons cream
1 tablespoon lemon juice
1 tablespoon chives, washed
1 bundle of asparagus, cleaned
Salt
Freshly ground black pepper
Water

*Home **brewing** has always been popular in Wales and many country folk still make their own wine with ingredients from the countryside and garden. An open basket is probably the best container for juicy blackberries, raspberries or elderberries. Remember to line the basket with plastic bags to stop the juice from dripping through.*

Flake the salmon into a bowl. Stir in the yoghurt, cream and lemon juice. Mix in the freshly ground black pepper.

Cook the asparagus in salted water gently for about 20 minutes until tender and drain. Snip the chives with a pair of scissors and stir into the mixture.

Serve the dip in small bowls with the asparagus spears and freshly washed local salad vegetables.

*Throughout Wales there is an abundance of sewin (sea trout) and the oyster, mussel and scallop beds have been reseeded, while young **lobsters** have been reintroduced into the Menai Straits.*

The spa at Llandrindod Wells is known for being the best medicinal waters in Wales. Pliny mentioned it as long ago as the first century. The Romans were known to have used the spa for helping to rid themselves of rheumatism.

MUSSELS IN WINE

1.5kg/3 lb mussels
$^1/_2$ bottle of dry white wine
450g/1 lb carrots, sliced
450g/ 1 lb potatoes, chopped
1 small swede, cleaned and chopped
2 large onions, sliced
2 cloves garlic, crushed
Bunch of mixed, fresh herbs
Salt and pepper
600ml/1 pint fish stock

*Laver, a lettuce-leaf type of **seaweed** is collected daily along the south coast. It is boiled and then sold from market stalls (such as in Swansea market) in the form of a gelatinous purée. Mixed with oatmeal, it is often served for breakfast with Welsh **bacon**.*

Discard any mussels that are open. Scrub the remaining mussels to remove any hairy beards and as many barnacles as possible. Place in a large pan with the stock. Add the wine and cover. Cook on high for 5 minutes until the shells open, stirring occasionally. Strain and reserve the liquid.

Heat the oil in a saucepan and add the onions, swede, potatoes, carrots and garlic. Cook for 5 minutes adding the herbs. Pour in the fish liquid and simmer, covered, for 5 minutes. Serve the mussels with hunks of fresh bread.

107

WELSH TOASTED CHEESE
(Tost Caws)

Take a slice of Welsh Caerphilly about 6mm/
$^1/_2$ inch thick and toast it on both sides. Do
not melt the cheese completely.

Toast a thick piece of bread on both sides
until crisp and spread very thinly with butter.

Place slices of raw onion on the bread, lay the
toasted cheese on the top and serve
immediately with a crisp green salad.

*Wales is ideal walking country, with Britain's only coastal national park. There are picturesque villages in unspoilt areas. Many local public houses offer good, traditional **home-cooked food** at reasonable prices.*

HOT SUMMER FRUITS

100g/4 oz raspberry jam
$^1/_2$ wineglass of rum
100g/4 oz strawberries
100g/4 oz raspberries
100g/4 oz blackcurrants
4 large plums
150ml/$^1/_4$ pint whipping cream
150ml/$^1/_4$ pint water

*Use an open basket if possible when gathering **mushrooms**. If they are put into a plastic bag they will sweat and go soggy.*

Melt the jam with a little water in a saucepan
and bring to the boil. Cut the plums into
quarters discarding the stones. Place in the
saucepan with the rest of the fruit. Mix
together gently (trying not to crush the
berries). Cook for 5 minutes.

Stir in the sugar and heat thoroughly until the
sugar has dissolved. Stir in the rum. Whip
the cream lightly and place on top of each
serving if desired.

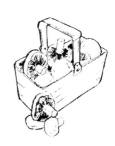

SEAFOOD SHELLS

*From Wednesday –
Sunday from mid June to
mid October a large
range of greenhouses,
peaches and herbs can be
seen in the Open Garden.
The walled kitchen
garden and the rest of the
14 acres overlooks the
estuary with its
exceptional views, rock
gardens and water
gardens. Located near
Aberystwyth on the
A493 and open from
2.30 - 5.30 pm, it is a
delightful place to spend
an afternoon.*

100g/4 oz mashed potato
1 teaspoon oil
1 onion, peeled and chopped
1 clove garlic, crushed
2 teaspoons parsley, chopped
100g/4 oz white fish, cooked
100g/4 oz cockles, shelled and rinsed
100g/4 oz prawns, cooked and shelled
Salt and pepper
25g/1 oz flour
25g/1 oz butter
300ml/$^1/_2$ pint milk

Heat the oil and cook the onion until soft. Put the butter into a saucepan on high, stir and cook for 1 minute. Gradually blend in the milk and cook until the sauce thickens.

Pipe the mashed potato around each shell and place under a hot grill until browned on the surface.

Fold the cockles, prawns and cooked white fish into the sauce. Season with salt, pepper, garlic and parsley. Continue to cook for 1 more minute. Spoon the fish mixture into the scallop shells.

*There is a legendary lake
at Aberdyfi, near
Aberystwyth which is
said to be the home of the
fairy milkmaid.*

110

CREAMY MUSHROOMS

100g/4 oz mushrooms, sliced thickly
1 teaspoon butter
150ml/$^1/_4$ pint sour cream
$^1/_2$ teaspoon salt,
Large pinch cayenne pepper

Cook the mushrooms in the butter in a pan for 10 minutes, stirring. When *just* tender, remove from the heat, allow to cool for a few minutes and stir in the cream.

Add the salt and cayenne and pour over cooked chicken breasts for a tasty snack.

Beaded jug covers can be bought at Hay-on-Wye. They are handmade from 100% cotton and are washable with coloured beads to weigh down the sides of the cover. Placed over a jug or dish they will keep out flies in the summer and are ideal for use in the kitchen or garden.

PARSNIP FRITTERS

450g/1 lb parsnips, cleaned
100g/4 oz flour, plus 1 tablespoon
1 egg
150ml/$^1/_4$ pint milk
Oil for shallow frying
Chopped basil
Pinch salt
4 tablespoon cold water

Chop the parsnips into rings and cook in boiling salted water for 10 minutes. Drain well. Stir the flour and salt together in a bowl. Add the egg and milk and beat until smooth.

Dip the parsnip rings in the remaining flour and then into the batter and fry in hot oil for 3 - 4 minutes each side, until golden brown. Drain on kitchen paper towel and serve immediately sprinkled with basil. These fritters can be served with boiled ham and green vegetables.

Look out for the 'Taste of Wales' symbol which is a sign of good food.

CHAPTER 10

The Children's Table

POTATO PATTIES

A widespread country belief was that the souls of the dead lived in the flower of the broad bean.

450g/1 lb potatoes,
25g/1 oz butter
2 tablespoons milk
100g/4 oz chopped bacon rashers
100g/4 oz breadcrumbs
1 tablespoon flour
Oil for frying
Salt and pepper
1 egg, beaten

Clean and boil the potatoes. Mash with the butter and milk. Add the bacon and season. Allow to cool and turn on to a lightly floured board. Form into even rounds and coat with the egg and breadcrumbs. Fry in the oil until golden brown.

*Micro tip:
The quickest way to make a jelly is to put the jelly cubes into a 600ml/1 pint jug and melt them on FULL in the microwave for 35 seconds. Make up to 600ml/1 pint with cold water and stir well. (You can add less water and a few ice cubes to set the jelly even faster).

DROP DOUGHNUTS

100g/4 oz white flour
50g/2 oz wholemeal flour
1 egg
1 teaspoon bicarbonate of soda
300ml/$^1/_2$ pint milk
Sugar
Oil for frying

Beat the egg into a basin, whisk in the milk and stir in the flour. Gently mix in the bicarbonate of soda.

Drop teaspoonfuls of the mixture into boiling hot fat and fry until golden brown. Drain on kitchen paper and roll in sugar.

112

HOME-MADE GINGER BEER

40g/1¹/₂ oz bruised ginger
3 lemons
25g/1 oz cream of tartar
450g/1 lb sugar
15g/¹/₂ oz fresh yeast
2 slices of toast
4.5 litres/8 pints water

The livestock and general market at Welshpool, Montgomeryshire is held on Mondays while the seasonal livestock market at nearby Llanfair Caereinion on Tuesdays are both well worth a visit.

Grate the rinds of the lemons and boil with a little of the water, ginger, sugar and cream of tartar. Pour into a large bowl and stir in the rest of the water. Spread the yeast on the toast and float on the top of the liquid. Cover with a large cloth and leave for 24 hours.

Strain and bottle the beer but cork loosely.. Leave for 3 days and strain again. The ginger beer will now be ready to use.

*At one time **Honey** was the most readily available sweetening agent.*

CREAMY HONEY FUDGE

450g/1 lb sugar
3 tablespoons honey
75g/3 oz butter plus 1 teaspoon
150ml/$\frac{1}{4}$ pint milk
$\frac{1}{2}$ teaspoon vanilla flavouring

*Micro tip:
Fresh breadcrumbs can be dried in the microwave for use in some of the recipes in this book.

Place the sugar, honey, butter and milk into a heavy saucepan. Heat gently and stir until the sugar dissolves. Boil until the temperature is 116C/240F. Remove the pan from the heat, add the vanilla flavouring and beat well with a wooden spoon.

Pour into a shallow square tin that has been greased and allow to set for 10 minutes. Mark into squares with a knife and leave to cool.

CHEESE STRAWS

100g/4 oz flour, sifted plus 3 tablespoons
75g/3 oz butter plus 1 teaspoon
75g/3 oz mature cheese, grated
Pinch of cayenne pepper
2 egg yolks, beaten
$^1/_2$ teaspoon salt

Pre-heat the oven to 160C/325F/Gas mark 3
and grease a baking tray. Rub the butter into
the flour until it resembles breadcrumbs. Mix
in the grated cheese, salt and cayenne pepper.
Bind together to a stiff dough with the egg
yolks.

Roll out the dough thinly and cut into strips.
Place on the prepared tray and bake until
crispy. Leave to cool for a few minutes before
transferring to a wire rack to cool.

*Micro tip:
Chocolate can be
melted so easily in the
microwave. Break the
pieces into a bowl and
melt on FULL for 1
minute. Use to spread
on cakes and cookies.

APPLE FRITTERS

100g/4 oz flour plus 1 tablespoon
1 egg, separated
4 tablespoons milk
3 tablespoons cold water
2 large cooking apples, peeled and sliced
75g/3 oz caster sugar
2 level teaspoons cinnamon
$^1/_2$ teaspoon salt
Oil for frying

Mix together the flour and salt. Beat in the
egg yolk, milk and water. Whisk the egg
white and fold into the batter. Pour oil into a
deep pan. Dust each slice of apple with the
flour. Dip into the batter mix and fry for 2
minutes. Drain on kitchen paper and dredge
with sugar and cinnamon. Serve while hot.

*In Wales, to carry a
rabbit's foot was once
said to guard from evil
and a newborn child was
supposed to be lucky in
life if brushed over with a
rabbit's foot within 10
days of the birth.*

115

FISH CAKES

450g/1 lb cooked white fish
25g/1 oz butter
Juice and rind of 1 lemon
2 tablespoons chopped parsley
1 egg, beaten
100g/4 oz fresh breadcrumbs plus
50g/2 oz fresh breadcrumbs
Oil for frying

Freshly made butter is still available from food stalls in the local markets of Wales.

Flake the fish with a fork to remove all bones. Mix with the breadcrumbs, butter and parsley. Bind together with the beaten egg.

Form into small cakes and coat with the breadcrumbs. Fry in oil until crisp and golden. Drain and keep warm while cooking the rest of the cakes.

MACAROONS

100g/4 oz ground almonds
100g/4 oz caster sugar
50g/2 oz desiccated coconut
$\frac{1}{4}$ teaspoon almond essence
Sheets of rice paper
1 egg

*Micro tip:
The microwave can be used for softening cream cheese. A few seconds on HIGH is useful when creaming butter or margarine used straight from the refrigerator.

Mix the almonds with the sugar, essence and egg to make a stiff paste. Take pieces of the mixture and form into small balls. Lay the rice paper on a baking sheet and press the almond balls on to it.

Bake in a pre-heated oven at 200C/400F/Gas mark 6 for 15 minutes. Remove from the oven and transfer to a wire rack to cool.

116

BREAD PUDDING

225g/8 oz stale bread
100g/4 oz raisins
100g/4 oz sultanas
50g/2 oz finely shredded suet
50g/2 oz sugar plus 1 tablespoon
50g/2 oz mixed peel
1 egg, beaten
1 teaspoon nutmeg
1 teaspoon cinnamon
1 teaspoon mixed spice
300ml/¹/₂ pint water
Milk

Visit Llangedwyn Mill, Llanfyllin, on the banks of the River Tanat to see the restored craft centre. There is a cafe and picnic area.

Break the bread into small pieces and cover it with milk and water. Leave to soak for an hour, then strain and squeeze out the liquid.

Break the lumps of bread with a fork and stir in the sugar, raisins, sultanas, peel, suet and spices. Add the egg and as much milk as needed to make the mixture moist enough to drop easily from the spoon. Spoon into a greased baking dish and bake for 1 hour at 180C/350F/Gas mark 4.

Test with a skewer to ensure the centre is cooked through. Sprinkle with the extra sugar and cut into chunks when cool.

When football first began it was a popular sport throughout the country including Wales. A blown-up pig's bladder was kicked about and any amount of people could join in the game.

117

CHAPTER 11
The Slimmer's Table

*Micro tip:
If your cup of coffee has gone cold, microwave for 30 seconds on full to heat it up again. Allow to stand for a few seconds as stirring immediately can cause the coffee to splash, causing burns.

TOMATO AND BASIL SALAD

1 very large tomato per person
2 tablespoons chopped fresh basil
2 teaspoons ground nut oil
Salt

Thinly slice the tomato and lay with the slices slightly overlapping each other in a dish. Sprinkle over the oil, a little salt if desired and the chopped basil. Cover and refrigerate for at least 1 hour.

GOOSEBERRY PARFAIT

225g/8 oz gooseberries, hulled
150ml/¼ pint low-fat plain yoghurt
Mint leaves to garnish
3 teaspoons honey
2 teaspoons powdered gelatine
150ml/¼ pint unsweetened apple juice
Water

Place the gooseberries, apple juice and honey into a saucepan and bring to the boil, stirring. Simmer for 15 minutes until the gooseberries are soft.

Blend in a liquidiser until puréed. Sprinkle the gelatine over a little hot water and stir until dissolved. Stir into the purée.

Blend in the yoghurt and pour into sundae dishes. Allow to set and garnish with the mint leaves.

*One of the world's largest secondhand bookshops is Booth's, Hay-on-Wye. It is worth browsing in the hope of finding a 'treasure' in the way of a **cookery** book, which may have been long since out-of-print.*

LEEKS IN YOGHURT SAUCE

8 slender leeks
Juice and rind of 1 lemon
Salt and pepper
Bunch of fresh coriander or basil
2 shallots, sliced
150ml/$^1/_4$ pint stock
150ml/$^1/_4$ pint natural yoghurt
3 egg yolks
1 teaspoon ready-made mustard
Parsley to garnish, chopped

The Dyfi Bridge which was built in 1805, crosses the salmon river – perfect for fishing – the River Dyfi, Machynlleth. The bridge marks the border between Meirionnydd and Montgomeryshire.

Put the stock, lemon rind and juice, coriander and shallots into a saucepan and bring to the boil. Season with salt and pepper. Trim the leeks and slit them halfway down each stem. Wash thoroughly and put the leeks in a frying pan. Strain the stock over them. Cover with a lid and simmer for 10 minutes until soft. Leave to cool in the liquid.

Beat the yoghurt, egg yolks and mustard together in a bowl and place over a pan of simmering water. Cook the sauce stirring all the time. Season with salt and pepper.

The traditional landscape of Wales is one of small fields, divided with stone walls and natural woodlands. The fields for hill farming are not fertile enough for growing crops. Hardy breeds of cattle and Welsh Mountain sheep have been introduced over the years.

Drain the leeks thoroughly, arrange on a serving plate and spoon over the yoghurt sauce. Serve with the chopped parsley.

119

BAKED TROUT

1 trout about 275g/10 oz per person
50g/2 oz breadcrumbs
Pinch of cayenne pepper
Large bunch of fresh herbs
50g/2 oz mushrooms, sliced
25g/1 oz crushed almonds
1 tablespoon fresh lemon juice
1 clove garlic, crushed
Juice of $\frac{1}{2}$ lemon
1 egg yolk, beaten
Oil

Wash the fish and dry with paper towels
thoroughly. Make 3 diagonal slashes on each
side of the fish. Sprinkle inside the cavity
with the lemon juice and dust with the
cayenne pepper.

Finely chop half of the herbs and combine
with the breadcrumbs and crushed almonds.
Brush one side of the fish with egg. Dip into
the herbed breadcrumbs. Place the rest of the
herbs in the cavity of the fish and secure with
several cocktail sticks if needed.

Coat the other side of the fish in the same
way. Brush a baking dish lightly with oil.
Place the sliced mushrooms in the bottom of
the dish and arrange the trout on the top.

*Micro tip:
Whilst seafood cooks
superbly in a
microwave oven, be
careful not to overcook
prawns, squid and
scallops as
overcooking will make
them tough.

Sprinkle with a little oil and bake, uncovered
at 200C/400F/Gas mark 6 for 25 minutes.

The fish should be lightly browned but not
burnt. Remove the cocktail sticks and serve
with a fresh, tomato and basil salad (see page
118).

POACHED CHICKEN BREASTS

2 boneless chicken breasts
2 carrots, peeled and diced
1 clove garlic, finely chopped
2 leeks, washed and chopped
300ml/$^1/_2$ pint chicken stock
1 glass white wine
Bunch of fresh herbs

Arrange the chicken breasts in a saucepan.
Combine the ingredients and pour over the
chicken. Bring to the boil, cover and simmer
for 25 minutes, turning once.

Turn off the heat and leave the chicken for 15
minutes before serving. Sprinkle with
chopped herbs and serve with boiled
potatoes, mashed carrots and a low calorie
dressing if desired.

*Black grouse, thought to
be fairly common in the
early eighteenth century,
feed primarily on heather
and* **bilberries**. *They
were fairly common on
the scrubby woodlands of
Snowdonia but slowly
declined and now
number as few as 1500
birds.*

St. David is the patron saint of Wales. St. David is also known as the patron of flocks and ships according to H.V. Morton (see 'In Search of Wales' published by Jarrold & Sons Ltd. 1963). St. David's Cathedral is known to be one of the oldest in Great Britain – it was founded about the year A.D. 550. St. David's day is celebrated on 1st March each year.

BAKED PEARS IN RED WINE

4 pears, firm, skinned
300ml/¹/₂ pint red wine
3 tablespoons honey
¹/₂ cinnamon stick
1 long strip lemon peel
¹/₂ teaspoon vanilla essence
4 cloves

*The Leat river teems with **mullet, salmon** and **sea trout**.*

Leaving the stalks on the pears, gradually peel each one from top to bottom in strips. Put a clove in the bottom of each pear, and place them in a casserole, standing upright.

Mix the wine, honey, vanilla and cinnamon stick, in a saucepan. Heat thoroughly to dissolve the honey. Pour over the fruit. Cover with foil and bake at 160C/325F/Gas mark 3 for 20 minutes, basting occasionally. Strain the juice and spoon a little over the pears. Remove the cloves and transfer to a serving dish. Serve chilled.

GRILLED HERRING

2 large herring
1 large onion, cut thickly
2 large carrots, cut thickly
Large bunch of fresh herbs
100g/4 oz oil
$\frac{1}{2}$ bottle dry white wine
Salt and pepper

Although cockles can be purchased in their shells they can be bought boiled or in jars ready for use.

Mix together the juice of the lemon, oil, salt and pepper and the white wine. Place the onion, carrot and herbs in the bottom of a large pan. Pour over the lemon and wine marinade and lay the herring on the top. Cover and leave in the refrigerator overnight turning once or twice if possible.

Remove the herring from the dish. Grill on both sides until brown and tender.

Place a little oil in a frying pan and cook the carrots and onions, removed from the marinade with a slotted spoon. Arrange the vegetables on a serving dish with the herrings and sauté potatoes.

The Welsh Black cattle are native to Wales and although traditionally they were reared to provide both milk and meat they are mostly used today as beef cattle. Many Welsh Blacks are to be seen on the working hill farms of Snowdonia.

ACKNOWLEDGEMENTS

I would like to thank Mr. D. Philip Davies and
Mr. Dewi Morris Jones, from the Welsh Books Council, Aberystwyth,
for their support in the initial idea, Alf for his continuing assistance
and undying belief in my abilities, Russ for his encouragement,
Norman for being there, and my family and friends who have tried,
tested and loaned their crockery and stomachs during testing and
photography in the making of this book.

Index

Index (continued)

ABOUT THE AUTHOR

Christine Smeeth has strong family ties with Wales and was brought up with a background of wholesome country cooking.

She trained as a Cordon Bleu Chef. After receiving many other qualifications she graduated as a home economist and stylist specialising in photographic shoots for the advertising and magazine markets and regularly works for such companies as Heinz, Weightwatchers and Birds Eye/Walls.

This is her sixth cookery book and she is a freelance contributor to many magazines enhancing her recipes with her own photography and illustrations.

She lives in Surrey and teaches for Surrey County Council but her roots are firmly embedded in Wales and the West Country, where she spends as much time as possible.